Lobster!

55 FRESH & SIMPLE RECIPES
for Everyday Eating

BROOKE DOJNY

Storey Publishing

The mission of Storey Publishing is to serve our customers by publishing practical information that encourages personal independence in harmony with the environment.

Edited by Margaret Sutherland
Art direction by Mary Winkelman Velgos
Book design and text production by woolypear

Photography by © Sabra Krock
Prop styling by Sabra Krock
Food styling by Mariana Velasquez
Illustrations by woolypear

Indexed by Christine R. Lindemer, Boston Road Communications

Storey books are available for special premium and promotional uses and for customized editions. For further information, please call 1-800-793-9396.

Storey Publishing
210 MASS MoCA Way
North Adams, MA 01247
www.storey.com

Printed in China by R.R. Donnelley
10 9 8 7 6 5 4 3 2 1

LIBRARY OF CONGRESS CATALOGING-IN-PUBLICATION DATA ON FILE

To lobster fishermen everywhere

CONTENTS

CHAPTER 5

ROLLS, TACOS, PIZZAS, AND SANDWICHES

CHAPTER 6

SIDES

CHAPTER 7

A LEMON, BERRY, OR CHOCOLATE FINISH

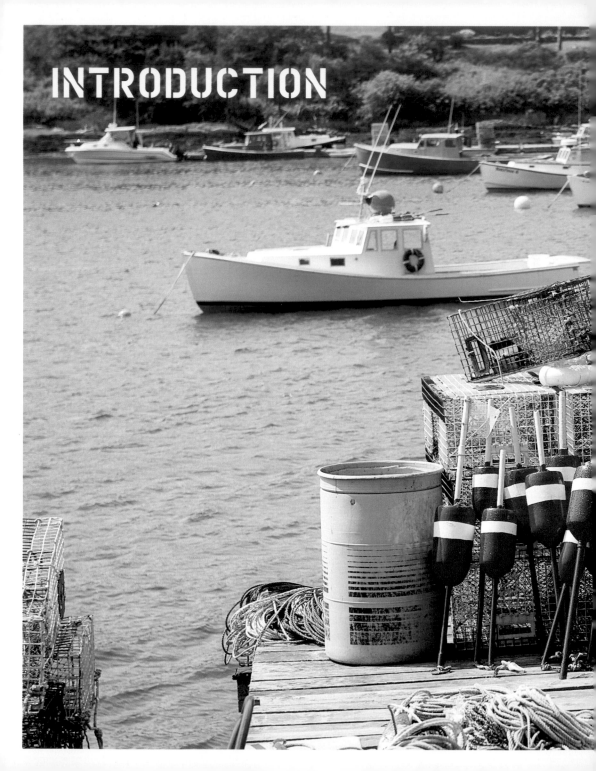

INTRODUCTION

Opulent. Primitive. Extravagant. Down-to-earth.

Beautiful. Ugly and buglike. The cardinal of the ocean. The jewel in seafood's crown. Lobster is a difficult food to describe. Mere words cannot come close to doing justice to the transcendent gustatory pleasure of eating a freshly steamed lobster — first cracking apart the gorgeous, bright red shell, then pulling out the briny-sweet, succulent pink and white meat, and adding a squirt of lemon juice and a gilding of melted butter. The taste is like extract of ocean.

The American or Maine lobster, *Homarus americanus*, found in the cold waters off the North Atlantic coast, is one of the most prized ingredients in the culinary world. *Homarus americanus,* a.k.a. "true" coldwater lobsters, are distinguished by their large, heavy, and very powerful claws. Spiny lobsters, also known as rock lobsters, live in warmer southeastern, southern Californian, and Caribbean waters and are sold mostly as frozen lobster tails. The rock lobster meat is not as flavorful or sweet as the meat of the Maine or American lobster fished out of cold waters. Crayfish and European langoustine are relatives.

Before the nineteenth century, lobsters were so abundant in New England that they could simply be plucked off the beach — but people who could afford not to, didn't. Lobsters were considered a low-class food in old New England, and prisoners were forced to eat them three times a week. Or they were fed to the chickens. In the mid-nineteenth century, fishermen began lobstering by boat, and by that time their relative scarcity increased demand. Fishing smacks, boats equipped with circulating wells of seawater holding thousands of pounds of lobsters, ferried the live crustaceans from Maine down to Boston's lobster-hungry populace.

Catching Lobsters

Lobsters, unlike most other seafood, must be kept alive until they are cooked, so ingenious Yankees have designed, crafted, and refined specialized techniques and gear for catching the "bugs." (See facing page for a long list of lobster lingo.)

Lobster Boats

The typical inshore lobster boat is a sturdy, deep-hulled vessel, 25 to 42 feet long, with an open deck and equipped with a hydraulic winch to haul heavy traps aboard. An independent fisherman will usually be out on the water for about half the year, setting traps in spring and hauling them out in late fall. Some fishermen work alone, but many have an assistant — a "sternman" (never a "sternwoman," even if the helper is female). Boats typically leave the dock at dawn, haul traps all day whatever the weather — up to 500 in a day — and stop at a wholesaler on the way home to sell the day's catch.

Lobster Traps

Lobster traps (or "pots") were fashioned out of wooden lath until late in the twentieth century. The basic trap design remains very much the same, although modern "pots" are constructed of vinyl-coated galvanized steel mesh which, unlike wood, does not rot and seldom breaks. The trap is a rectangular box with an entrance and two "rooms," separated by woven netting. The lobster enters the first room, the baited "kitchen," and passes into the next room, the "parlor" or "bedroom," from which it is difficult to exit.

LOBSTER LINGO

Bands Rubber bands that lobster fishermen snap onto the pincher and crusher claws to prevent the creatures from slashing humans or each other with their sharp claws.

Berries Fertilized lobster eggs attached to the underside of a female lobster.

Bugs An affectionate term for all lobsters.

Buoy Float that marks the line leading to a lobster trap. Each fisherman has his own signature buoy markings.

Cars Crates to store lobsters just offshore until they go to market.

Chicken A 1-pound lobster.

Cock A male lobster.

Coral Unfertilized roe in a female lobster. Found throughout the tail, it is shiny and black when raw and turns a bright coral red when cooked.

Crusher The larger, stronger claw with coarser teeth.

Cull A lobster missing one or both claws.

Hen A female lobster.

Keeper A lobster measuring 3¼ to 5 inches from the eye sockets to the top of the tail, the legal limits for market.

Kitchen The first chamber of a lobster trap, where the lobster goes to eat the bait.

Parlor The inner chamber of a lobster trap. Also known as the bedroom, this is where the lobster is confined to await the lobster fisherman.

Ripper The smaller of the two large claws, with finer teeth.

Shedder A newly molted lobster. It has absorbed seawater into its body and has extra space in its soft shell.

Short A lobster that falls below the legal size.

Smellers Another name for lobster antennae.

Sternman Assistant to the captain of a lobster boat.

Trap Sometimes also called a "pot," modern traps are usually made of heavy, plastic-coated wire instead of the traditional wood.

Lobster Fishery

Commercial lobster fishing is a healthy industry in the cold waters off northern New England and Maritime Canada. Maine supplies the bulk of American lobsters, and the industry is largely self-regulated to protect the fishery for future generations. Laws prohibit fishermen from taking undersize or oversize lobsters and breeding ("berried") females.

Buying and Cooking Lobsters

If you can't buy them off a fishing boat (and most people can't), purchase live lobsters from a lobster co-op or lobster company, where lobsters are stored in submerged crates, pounds, or pools, or in large tanks filled with circulating seawater. Fish and seafood markets, particularly busy ones that turn over inventory quickly, are another good source. If buying from a supermarket, make sure the tank is clean and uncrowded, and that the lobsters are lively. A healthy lobster should flip its tail and kick its legs vigorously when lifted up. Live lobsters can be mail-ordered if they're not available where you live (see Mail Order Websites, page 137).

Cooked lobsters and picked-out meat can be had at seafood markets, but it's a good idea to call ahead to request what you need. Frozen cooked lobster and raw meat extracted in water-filled compression chambers are becoming more available, too. Both options are convenient but pricey; it's much cheaper to buy live or cooked whole lobsters and pick out the meat yourself.

Hard-Shell vs. Soft-Shell

Lobsters molt (shed their shells) several times per year. After molting, the lobster's shell begins to harden and the meat grows to fill the new shell. Because of the timing of their life cycle, most lobsters trapped during the summer months are newly molted soft-shells, or are at some stage in the process between soft- and hard-shelled. Very soft-shelled lobsters ("shedders") are watery, with underdeveloped, somewhat spongy claw meat. Very hard-shelled lobsters are packed with meat, but their shells are so calcified that major carpentry is required to open them. I prefer to eat lobsters that are somewhere in between their molting stages (sometimes referred to as "new-shells"), when they're still easy to dismantle but have plenty of sweet meat. If buying lobsters to travel, choose hard-shells. Soft-shells are too frail to withstand much time out of circulating salt water.

Storing Live Lobsters

Lobsters must be alive when they go into the pot because when they die they release gastric enzymes that begin to deteriorate the meat. If you will be cooking lobsters within a few hours, store them in a bag in the coldest part of the refrigerator or in a cooler. Do not store on ice or in tap water. For overnight storage, loosely wrap lobsters individually in damp newspaper — Mainers always dampen with seawater — and place in the coldest part of the refrigerator (usually the bottom shelf). Hard-shells can be stored for a day or so; soft-shells are more perishable and often die if held overnight.

What Pot?

Bigger is better. A large enamel canning pot is ideal for cooking four or five lobsters, but any large (4- to 5-quart capacity) pot will do. Or use two or three smaller pots. Do not crowd the pots or the lobsters will not perish as quickly and will not cook as evenly.

Numbing

Sticking the live lobsters in the freezer for about 30 minutes before cooking numbs them so they are more docile when they hit the heat.

Steaming vs. Boiling

Lobsters can be boiled in a large pot of salted water or steamed in a small amount of water. I generally prefer steaming, especially when cooking soft-shells. Steaming has several advantages: it is safer and easier than dealing with a large pot of boiling water; the water returns to a boil faster so timing is more accurate; it's less messy because there are fewer boil-overs; and, most important, the lobsters have better flavor because they're less diluted with water. However, boiling is the better option when cooking more than three or four hard-shell lobsters because the heat circulates more evenly around the lobsters.

Cooking

See the cooking instructions for Plain Steamed or Boiled Lobster on page 59. If cooking lobster for the meat only, immediately plunge the hot lobsters into a large bowl of ice water to stop the cooking and then pick out the meat.

Use this chart only as a guideline. Soft-shell lobsters vary widely and can yield lesser amounts than shown. Hard-shell lobsters take the longer cooking times and yield the larger and more consistent amounts of meat. **If in doubt, buy an extra soft-shell lobster or two.**

LOBSTER SIZE	COOKING TIME	MEAT YIELD
1 pound	9–11 minutes	2½–4 ounces (¾ cup)
1¼ pounds	12–15 minutes	4–5 ounces (1 cup)
1½ pounds	14–17 minutes	5½–8 ounces (1½ cups)
1¾–2 pounds	17–19 minutes	6½–10 ounces (1¾ cups)

NOTE: *If meat is finely chopped, the cup measurement will be about one-quarter less than this chart indicates.*

Quick Lobster Broth

For a simple homemade lobster broth, split three cooked lobster bodies and remove the head sacs up near the eyes. Place in a large stockpot along with any leftover lobster shells and some tomalley, if desired. Cover with about 10 cups water, add 2 teaspoons salt, and bring to a boil. Skim off the foam that rises to the surface and simmer uncovered for 30 minutes. Strain through a medium-mesh sieve.

Even Quicker Lobster Broth

If you have lobster cooking water you can use it for broth. Strain out any extraneous matter. If it is too salty, dilute with water. (If you plan to use cooking water for broth, rinse the lobsters under cold water before cooking.)

Purchased Seafood Broth/Stock and Clam Juice

Since there is no official culinary differentiation between broth and stock, I have chosen to use the term "broth" in this book. Look for commercial seafood broth/stock, usually sold in 1-quart cartons, near the canned chicken and beef broths in the supermarket. Bottled clam juice, usually shelved with the canned fish, is another alternative. Dilute clam juice with water if it's too salty.

Splitting a Live Lobster

This procedure is not as difficult as it sounds, though it is much easier with soft-shell lobsters. Place lobsters in the freezer for 20 to 30 minutes to numb them. Wearing rubber or work gloves, place the lobster on a cutting board shell side up. Grasp the tail.

[1]

1. There is a cross-mark on the top of every lobster shell near the head. Insert the point of a sharp, sturdy knife into this mark and plunge the knife straight down into the body. The lobster may do some reflexive twitching, but it is dead.

2. Now, with one swift motion, split the lobster body in half lengthwise through the head.

3. Turn underside up and cut through the body and the tail.

[3]

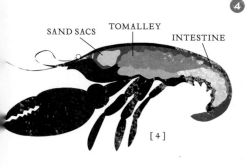

SAND SACS   TOMALLEY   INTESTINE

[4]

④ Discard the intestinal vein and the sand sacs in the head near the eyes. Remove most of the runny yellow-gray tomalley. Pull off the rubber bands. If the lobsters are hard-shell, use a hammer to crack the claws so that heat can better penetrate. Cook within about 1 hour.

Parboiling a Lobster

Parboiling is a good option if splitting live lobsters seems too daunting. Bring a large pot of water to a boil and add 2 tablespoons salt. Drop the lobsters headfirst into the boiling water, cover, and cook just until bright red, 3 to 5 minutes, depending on size. Remove with tongs and plunge into a large bowl of ice water to stop the cooking, and then follow directions above to split, clean, and prepare for further cooking. Finish cooking within about 4 hours.

Keeping Cooked Lobster

Remove cooked meat from the shell, wrap well, and store in the coldest part of the refrigerator for up to two days. To freeze, place the meat in a plastic container or freezer bag, cover with whole milk, and freeze for up to six weeks.

How to Eat a Whole Lobster

1. Grasp the cooked lobster with one hand on the body and one hand on the tail and twist to break in two. Expect a gush of liquid on your plate. Drain it out into the debris bowl for shells on the table (an essential).

2. Start with the tail. First remove the flat flippers at the end and pull each one through your teeth like an artichoke leaf. Then poke the tail meat out with your finger, or, if the tail has been split, pull it apart with two hands and extract the meat. Remove and discard the black vein running down the center. Dip the meat into melted butter and eat.

3. Twist off the entire large pincher claw legs where they meet the body. Twist off the pincher claws. Using a nutcracker, crack the claws and the knuckles. The claw meat is easy to get at; sometimes you have to poke out the knuckle meat — some of the sweetest — with a lobster pick or your little finger.

For the persistent person, there are still the small legs, again best eaten by running through your teeth; there are also small nuggets of meat in the joints where the legs meet the body.

CHAPTER ONE

HORS D'OEUVRES

Lobster Cocktails

Cocktail Sauce

½ cup chili sauce
or ketchup

1½ tablespoons prepared
horseradish, or to taste

2 teaspoons lemon juice

~~~~~~~~~~~~~~~~~~

Lobster

12 ounces picked-out
lobster meat, tails and claws
intact (see Note)

1¼ cups shredded
iceberg lettuce

4 lemon slices for garnish

~~~~~~~~~~~~~~~~~~

4 SERVINGS

Ryan Dorr, a third-generation lobster fisherman out of Stonington, Maine, prepares this appetizer as a special treat for his family at Christmastime. I've written the recipe as individual lobster cocktails to serve four, but since Ryan is usually serving ten or more, he presents the well-chilled lobster chunks on a bed of ice and hangs halved tails over the bowl of spicy cocktail sauce "like candy canes."

1. To make the sauce, stir together the chili sauce, horseradish, and lemon juice. Taste and add more horseradish if you like. Refrigerate for at least 1 hour or for up to 2 days.

2. Chill four stemmed 6-ounce cocktail glasses, such as large martini glasses.

3. To prepare the lobster, split the tails in half lengthwise and remove the black vein. Trim the ragged bottoms of four half-tails to resemble jumbo shrimp. Split the intact claws in half lengthwise to retain their distinctive shape. Cut the remaining lobster meat into bite-size chunks.

4. Nestle the shredded lettuce in the bottoms of the glasses. Arrange the lobster chunks over the lettuce, place claws on top, and hang a trimmed lobster tail over the side of each glass. Garnish with a lemon slice. Refrigerate for at least 1 hour to chill thoroughly.

5 Place each stemmed glass on a small plate and pass the cocktail sauce for spooning over the lobster.

NOTE: *Cook three 1¼-pound soft-shell lobsters and remove the meat (see chart, page 15) or purchase cooked intact lobster claws and tails.*

LARRY, THE RHODE ISLAN' MONSTAH LOBSTAH

"Our family was at dinner at the Wharf Tavern in Warren, Rhode Island, a couple of years ago. The waiter announced that they had a special that night . . . an eighteen-pound lobster that could feed our entire table for $125. After a great deal of family discussion, my husband, Keith, called the waiter over and told him we'd like to order the lobster . . . but we wanted it live! *We dubbed him (or her?) Larry the Lobster. A couple of people at tables around us heard the conversation and chipped in to help us save Larry. We returned the next day with a cooler, packed Larry up, and drove 50 miles to the Mystic Aquarium, where we'd arranged to donate Larry and where he lives on happily in one of their large tanks. The story about our lobster rescue mission ran in our local newspaper, and months later I met a woman who told me that her young son was so moved by Larry's plight that he insisted on being taken to Mystic to meet Larry in person."*

Susan Maloney, Bristol, Rhode Island

Mini Lobster Cakes

with Lime-Pepper Aioli

Aioli

1/2 cup mayonnaise

1 teaspoon grated lime zest

2 tablespoons lime juice

1 teaspoon finely
minced garlic

1/2 teaspoon freshly
ground black pepper

~~~~~~~~~~~~~~~~

Lobster Cakes

1 small egg (see Note)

3/4 cup finely crushed
saltine crackers

1/4 cup mayonnaise

3 tablespoons minced
scallions, white
and green parts

1 teaspoon lime juice

1/2 teaspoon
Worcestershire sauce

1/4 teaspoon Old Bay
Seasoning or similar
seafood seasoning mix

Ingredients continue opposite

Tiny lobster cakes are served with a garlicky lime-pepper-spiked aioli dipping sauce to make a quite spectacular hors d'oeuvre. The cakes can be made ahead and frozen.

1. To make the aioli, whisk together the mayonnaise, lime zest and juice, garlic, and pepper. Refrigerate for at least 2 hours or up to 3 days.

2. To make the lobster cakes, lightly beat the egg in a medium bowl. Add the cracker crumbs, mayonnaise, scallions, lime juice, Worcestershire, and Old Bay Seasoning, and blend well. Pulse the lobster meat in a food processor until finely chopped, add to the bowl, and mix thoroughly to combine.

3. Form the lobster mixture into about 30 tiny patties, using a scant tablespoon for each cake, and place the patties on a waxed paper–lined baking sheet. Cover and refrigerate for at least 2 hours. (The cakes can be made up to 24 hours ahead.)

4. Heat 2 tablespoons of the oil in a large skillet. Cook the cakes in batches over medium heat until golden brown and crisp on both sides and hot inside, 4 to 5 minutes total. Repeat with the remaining cakes, adding more oil as needed. (If not serving immediately, place on a foil-lined baking sheet,

wrap well, and refrigerate for up to 24 hours, or freeze. Remove from the refrigerator or freezer one hour before baking and reheat in a preheated 375-degree oven until hot and crisp, 8 to 10 minutes.)

5 Arrange the cakes on a serving platter accompanied by a small bowl of the aioli for dipping. Garnish the platter with lime slices.

NOTES:

1. If you don't have a small egg, whisk a large egg and scoop out half for this recipe.

2. Cook one 1½-pound hard-shell lobster or two 1-pound lobsters and remove the meat (see chart, page 15) or purchase picked-out meat.

1½ cups roughly chopped
cooked lobster meat
(8 ounces) (see Note)

2-3 tablespoons
vegetable oil

Thin lime slices for garnish

MAKES ABOUT 30 TINY
CAKES, 6-8 SERVINGS

FIRST TRAPS

The lobster trap was invented in 1808 by Ebenezer Thorndike of Swampscott, Massachusetts.

Lobster and Mango Salad
in Garlic Toast Cups

This very elegant hors d'oeuvre takes a little advance planning, but it's worth it. You'll need some mini-muffin tins to make the tiny toast cups, but they're very easy to do and can be made ahead. The lobster and mango salad is seasoned with a tiny amount of curry powder, which adds an elusive hint of flavor, as does the garlic butter that gets brushed on the toast cups.

1. Preheat the oven to 350 degrees.

2. Melt the butter with the garlic in a small saucepan. Cut the crusts off the bread and use a rolling pin to flatten each slice. Using a 2½-inch fluted or plain round cookie cutter, cut rounds out of the bread. Brush mini-muffin tins with the garlic butter, press the bread rounds into the bottom and sides of the tins, and brush the bread cups with more butter.

3. Bake the bread cups for 9 to 11 minutes, until golden brown. Remove the cups from the pans and cool on wire racks. (The cups can be stored in a tightly covered container at room temperature for 1 day or frozen. Return to room temperature before filling.)

4. Combine the cream cheese, mayonnaise, red onion, lime juice, and curry powder in a small bowl and whisk to blend. Add the lobster meat and stir to

Recipe continues on next page

4 tablespoons butter

1 small garlic clove, crushed

1 loaf Pepperidge Farm Very Thin white bread, or other thinly sliced white bread

3 tablespoons cream cheese, softened

1 tablespoon mayonnaise

3 tablespoons finely chopped red onion

1 tablespoon lime juice

½ teaspoon curry powder

1 cup finely diced cooked lobster meat (about 5 ounces) (see Note)

⅓ cup finely diced mango

½ teaspoon salt

¼ teaspoon freshly ground black pepper

Paprika

MAKES ABOUT
30 HORS D'OEUVRES

combine. (The salad can be made to this point up to 4 hours ahead and refrigerated.)

5 When ready to fill, fold the mango into the salad and season with the salt and pepper. Spoon a heaping teaspoon of lobster salad into each cup, sprinkle with a light dusting of paprika, and serve.

NOTES:

1. Small bite-size phyllo cups are a good substitute for the toast cups. Athena brand cups, found in the frozen food section, are good.

2. Cook one 1¼-pound hard-shell lobster or two 1-pound soft-shells and remove the meat (see chart, page 15) or buy picked-out meat.

ICONIC LOBSTERS

"Lobsters make for an unlikely icon.... In basic design, Homarus americanus resembles a self-propelled Swiss Army knife, with deployable appendages for every occasion."

Colin Woodard,
The Lobster Coast

Lobster and Melon Skewers

Chunks of pink-tinged lime- and garlic-marinated lobster meat are skewered with cubes of melon to make a startlingly beautiful single-bite hors d'oeuvre. Present on a platter or on shaved ice in a shallow bowl or stick the skewer points into half a melon.

1. Whisk together the oil, lime zest and juice, garlic, salt, cayenne, and chopped cilantro in a medium bowl. Add the lobster meat and stir to combine. Marinate in the refrigerator for at least 1 hour or for up to 4 hours.

2. When ready to assemble, thread short (5-inch) skewers (see Note) with one piece of melon, a slice of lime, and a chunk of lobster. Arrange on a platter. (Can be assembled up to 1 hour ahead and refrigerated, covered.) Garnish with cilantro sprigs before serving.

NOTES:

1. Cook two 1¼-pound hard-shell lobsters or three 1-pound soft-shells and remove the meat (see chart, page 15) or buy picked-out meat.

2. To make the lime wedges, cut a lime in half lengthwise and cut several very thin crosswise slices. Cut each slice into very tiny triangles less than ½-inch wide.

3. If you can't find short skewers, use garden clippers to cut longer bamboo skewers into shorter lengths.

¼ cup olive oil

1 teaspoon grated lime zest

1½ tablespoons lime juice

1 garlic clove, minced

½ teaspoon salt

¼ teaspoon cayenne pepper

2 tablespoons chopped fresh cilantro, plus sprigs for garnish

2 cups cooked lobster meat, cut into ¾-inch chunks (about 10 ounces) (see Note)

About 40 (¾-inch) cubes honeydew melon or cantaloupe, from about one-quarter of a melon

About 40 tiny triangles of thinly sliced lime (see Note)

MAKES ABOUT 40 SMALL SKEWERS, 6–8 SERVINGS

Mini Lobster Rolls

1½ cups finely diced cooked lobster meat (8 ounces) (see Note)

¼ cup mayonnaise

2 tablespoons minced scallions, white and green parts

1 teaspoon grated lemon zest

1 tablespoon lemon juice

½ teaspoon salt

¼ teaspoon freshly ground black pepper

About 7 top-split hot dog rolls

6 tablespoons butter, melted

About 28 small butter lettuce leaves, cut to fit inside rolls if necessary

~~~~~~~~~~~~~~~~~

MAKES ABOUT 28 MINI ROLLS, 4–6 SERVINGS

People adore these single-bite mini lobster rolls. The salad filling is similar to the one in a full-size roll, except that the seasonings are punched up just a tad.

1. Combine the lobster meat in a bowl with the mayonnaise, scallions, and lemon zest and juice. Season with the salt and pepper and stir well to combine. Refrigerate for at least 1 hour to blend flavors (can be made up to 4 hours ahead).

2. Preheat a griddle or cast-iron pan over medium heat. Cut the hot dog rolls crosswise into 1½-inch pieces. Brush the outsides of the rolls generously with melted butter and place on the griddle. Cook, turning once, until both cut sides are pale golden brown, about 1 minute per side.

3. Arrange a lettuce leaf in the bottom of each mini-roll, allowing the edges to overhang a bit, and fill with about 1 tablespoon of the lobster salad. Arrange the rolls on a platter and serve.

NOTE: *Cook one 1½-pound hard-shell lobster or two 1-pound soft-shells and remove the meat (see chart, page 15) or buy picked-out meat.*

Gratin of Lobster and Spinach

with Black Pepper Toasts

Gratin

1 (6-ounce) bag
baby spinach (see Note)

1 (8-ounce) package cream
cheese, softened

1/3 cup mayonnaise

2 tablespoons minced onion

1 teaspoon
Worcestershire sauce

1/2 teaspoon liquid
hot pepper sauce

1 teaspoon lobster tomalley,
if available (optional)

1 1/2 cups cooked lobster
meat, chopped medium-fine
(8 ounces) (see Note)

2 tablespoons grated
Parmesan cheese

~~~~~~~~~~~~~~~~~~

Ingredients continue opposite

A layer of cooked spinach nestles under this rich lobster-studded cream cheese blend. Served warm, the gratinéed lobster is surrounded by black pepper toasts for spreading. If you have tomalley from a cooked lobster, a small spoonful injects a real boost of lobster flavor.

1. Cook the spinach in a small amount of water in a saucepan or in the microwave just until wilted, about 3 minutes. Drain well and chop. You should have about 1/2 cup. Spread the spinach in the bottom of a shallow 1-quart ovenproof serving dish, such as an oval gratin dish.

2. Beat the cream cheese with the mayonnaise, onion, Worcestershire, and hot pepper sauce in a bowl. (It's easiest to do this using an electric mixer.) Stir in the tomalley, if desired, and fold in the lobster meat. Dollop the lobster mixture over the spinach and smooth the top. Sprinkle with the Parmesan, wrap, and refrigerate for at least 4 hours or for up to 24 hours. Bring to room temperature before baking.

3. To make the toasts, preheat the oven to 400 degrees. Cut about 30 thin (1/8-inch) slices from the baguette and arrange on a baking sheet. If the bread is more

than 1½ inches in diameter, cut the slices in half. Brush the slices with oil and grind black pepper over. Bake for 5 to 7 minutes, until the toasts are a pale golden brown. Cool. (The toasts can be stored in an airtight container for 1 day or frozen.)

4 To bake the gratin, preheat the oven to 375 degrees. Bake the gratin 20 to 25 minutes, until it is hot throughout and the top is lightly browned. Place the dish on a platter, surround with toasts, and serve.

NOTES:

1. You may substitute ½ cup thawed chopped frozen spinach, squeezed dry.

2. Cook one 1½-pound hard-shell lobster or two 1-pound soft-shells and remove the meat (see chart, page 15) or buy picked-out meat.

(see chart, page 15)

Toasts

1 skinny baguette

2 tablespoons olive oil

Freshly ground
black pepper

8–10 SERVINGS

LOBSTER TV

Cameras are set up on Maine's sea bottom to spy on lobsters at home. You can watch the bugs in their habitat on YouTube, www.downeast.com, and on several other websites. Voyeurism at its best!

Potted Lobster Mousse

¾ cup roughly chopped cooked lobster meat (3–4 ounces) (see Note)

⅓ cup whipped cream cheese

4 tablespoons cold butter, cut into small chunks, plus 1 tablespoon, melted

2 teaspoons grated lemon zest

2 teaspoons lemon juice

½ teaspoon liquid hot pepper sauce

3 tablespoons snipped fresh chives, plus spears for garnish

Salt

Crackers, for serving

~~~~~~~~~~~~~~~~

MAKES ¾ CUP, ABOUT 6 APPETIZER SERVINGS

This lovely creamy mousse is an excellent way to turn a bit of leftover cooked lobster into a simple and delicious appetizer. "Potted" is an old British culinary term for a method of preserving perishable food (especially seafood) in melted butter. Although these days we have refrigerators and freezers for that purpose, I still like the old name.

1. Pulse the lobster meat in a food processor until finely chopped and remove to a bowl; do not wash the processor.

2. Combine the cream cheese, cold butter, lemon zest and juice, and hot pepper sauce in the food processor and pulse until well blended. Add the lobster and pulse until quite smooth. Transfer to a bowl, stir in the snipped chives, and season with salt to taste.

3. Scrape the mixture into a ramekin and pour a thin layer of melted butter over to seal.

4. Refrigerate for at least 4 hours to allow the flavors to blend. (The ramekin can be filled up to 2 days ahead.)

5. Remove the ramekin from the refrigerator about 2 hours before serving. Garnish the mousse with chives and spread onto crackers to serve.

NOTE: *Cook one 1-pound hard-shell lobster and remove the meat (see chart, page 15) or buy picked-out meat.*

CHAPTER TWO

SALADS

OUR.
ZUCCHINI
green + yellow
$2/lb.

OUR
BEETS
$3/bunch

OUR
EGGPLANT
$2/lb.

Composed Lobster and Papaya Salad

with Toasted Cumin Vinaigrette

Papaya lends sweetness and pretty color to this gorgeous composed salad flavored with tropical seasonings. Accompany with toasted flatbread and Rustic Summer Fruit Tart (page 119) for an impressive and delicious summer lunch or supper.

1. To make the vinaigrette, toast the cumin in a small skillet over medium heat, stirring now and then, until one shade darker, 3 to 4 minutes. Combine the cumin with the vinegar, shallots, mustard, jalapeño, and lime zest in a small bowl. Whisk in the oil and season with the salt and pepper. (Can be made up to 2 days ahead and refrigerated.)

2. To make the salad, toss the lobster meat with about 2 tablespoons of the dressing. In another bowl, toss the tomatoes with about 2 tablespoons of the dressing. Refrigerate for 1 to 2 hours.

3. Spread the arugula out on a serving platter. Arrange the papaya, bell pepper, and avocado in separate but overlapping sections toward the edge of the platter. Scatter the dressed tomatoes over all. Heap the dressed lobster in the center and sprinkle the cilantro over the top. (Can be made up to 2 hours ahead and refrigerated.)

Vinaigrette

1 tablespoon ground cumin

3 tablespoons white wine vinegar

2 tablespoons minced shallots

1 tablespoon coarse-grain Dijon mustard

1 tablespoon minced pickled jalapeño pepper, or to taste

1 teaspoon grated lime zest

1/3 cup olive oil

1/2 teaspoon salt

1/4 teaspoon freshly ground black pepper

Salad

1 1/2 cups roughly chopped cooked lobster meat (8 ounces) (see Note)

1 1/2 cups halved grape or tiny plum tomatoes

Ingredients continue opposite

4 Drizzle with dressing, garnish with lime wedges, and serve.

NOTE: *Cook one 1½-pound hard-shell lobster or two 1-pound soft-shells and remove the meat (see chart, page 15) or purchase picked-out meat.*

~~~~~~

LINDA L. BEAN, LOBSTER ENTREPRENEUR

Linda L. Bean, granddaughter of famed Maine retailer L.L. Bean, runs several lobster-related businesses including lobster wharves and lobster pounds in midcoast Maine, a plant that processes lobsters caught by local fishermen, a huge restaurant in Freeport (Linda Bean's Maine Kitchen & Topside Tavern), and a café at the Portland airport.

~~~~~~

4 handfuls arugula

½ papaya,
seeded and sliced

½ red bell pepper, cut into
thin rings then halved

1 avocado, peeled, pitted
and sliced

½ cup fresh cilantro sprigs

Lime wedges for garnish

~~~~~~~~~~~~~~~~~~~~~

4 SERVINGS

Lobster and Pea Shoot Salad

with Creamy Mustard Dressing

The sweet, herbaceous flavor of young peas and pea shoots complements the lobster in this lovely springtime luncheon salad. Warm corn muffins or cornbread squares would be a nice accompaniment. Finish with Mocha–Chocolate Chip Shortbread Cookies (page 130) and berries.

1. To make the dressing, whisk the mayonnaise with the sour cream, lemon juice, and mustard in a small bowl. (Can be made up to one day ahead and refrigerated.)

2. Cook the bacon in a skillet over low heat until the fat is rendered and the bacon is crisp, 10 to 15 minutes, (or cook it in a microwave). Remove the bacon with a slotted spoon and drain on paper towels.

3. If using fresh peas, blanch them in a saucepan of boiling salted water until just tender, about 5 minutes. Drain, refresh in a bowl of ice water to stop the cooking, and drain again. If using frozen peas, simply run them under warm water to thaw and drain on paper towels.

4. Toss the lobster meat with the peas, tomatoes, and onion. Drizzle on enough dressing to bind the salad and season with salt and pepper to taste, keeping in

Recipe continues on next page

Dressing

⅓ cup mayonnaise

⅓ cup sour cream

2 tablespoons lemon juice

1 tablespoon coarse-grain Dijon mustard

~~~~~~~~~~~~~~~~~~

Salad

4 strips bacon

1 cup small peas, fresh or thawed frozen

2 cups chopped cooked lobster meat (10 ounces) (see Note)

1 medium tomato, seeded and diced

¼ cup finely chopped red onion

Salt and freshly ground black pepper

About 1½ cups tender pea shoots (see Note)

About 8 Romaine lettuce leaves

~~~~~~~~~~~~~~~~~~

4 SERVINGS

mind that the bacon will add a bit more saltiness. (Can be made up to 4 hours ahead and refrigerated.)

5 Line a serving platter with pea shoots. Fill lettuce leaves with the lobster salad and arrange over the pea shoots. Finely chop the bacon and sprinkle over the salad. Garnish with more pea shoots and serve.

NOTES:

1. Cook two 1¼-pound hard-shell lobsters or three 1-pound soft-shells and remove the meat (see chart, page 15) or purchase picked-out meat.

2. Pea shoots are becoming more available at farmers' markets and specialty markets, but if you can't get them, baby spinach is a good substitute.

SMART LOBSTER SHOPPING

Ask for "culls" (single- or no-claw lobsters), when you need only lobster meat. Culls are much cheaper than intact lobsters.

Tangy Tarragon Lobster Salad in Its Shell

If you have lobster shells, save four tail shells from split lobsters to use as pretty serving vessels for this simple, tangy, tarragon-flavored salad. To complete a summer luncheon or supper pass a basket of buttery dinner rolls and offer individual Strawberry Shortcakes (page 124) for dessert.

1. Whisk the mayonnaise with the chopped tarragon and cayenne in a small bowl.

2. Combine the lobster meat with the celery and capers in a bowl. Pour the mayonnaise mixture over the lobster mixture, toss to combine, and taste for seasoning, adding a pinch more cayenne if you like more heat. (Can be made up to 4 hours ahead and refrigerated.)

3. If serving in the shells, line each tail shell with a lettuce leaf and fill with salad. (If not using shells, simply place the lettuce leaves on a platter.) Garnish with tarragon sprigs and serve.

NOTE: *Cook two 1¼-pound hard-shell lobsters or three 1-pound soft-shells and remove the meat (see chart, page 15) or purchase picked-out meat.*

½ cup mayonnaise

2 tablespoons chopped fresh tarragon, plus sprigs for garnish

¼ teaspoon cayenne pepper, or to taste

2 cups chopped cooked lobster meat (10 ounces) (see Note)

½ cup finely chopped celery

1½ tablespoon drained capers

4 large leaves Boston, Bibb, or other soft lettuce

4 clean tail shell halves from 1-pound lobsters, if available (optional)

4 SERVINGS

Seashell Lobster Pasta Salad
with Lemon-Dill Cream

Cream

3/4 cup mayonnaise

1 tablespoon Dijon mustard

2 teaspoons grated lemon zest

1 tablespoon lemon juice

Salt and freshly ground black pepper

1 1/2 tablespoons chopped fresh dill

~~~~~~~~~~~~~~~~

Salad and Garnishes

10 ounces small or medium pasta shells

1 small yellow bell pepper, seeded and chopped

3/4 cup thinly sliced celery

1/2 cup chopped red onion

1 1/2 cups chopped cooked lobster meat (7-8 ounces) (see Note)

Ingredients continue opposite

Seashell pasta is the perfect shape for a lobster pasta salad. Not only are the shells reminiscent of the ocean, but they're also ideal for catching plenty of the lemon-dill cream. Add a basket of seeded French bread and serve Mocha–Chocolate Chip Shortbread Cookies (page 130) and bunches of green grapes for dessert.

1. Bring a large pot of salted water to a boil for the pasta.

2. To make the lemon-dill cream, whisk the mayonnaise with the mustard, lemon zest, and lemon juice in a small bowl. Season with salt and pepper to taste. Stir in the dill. (Can be prepared up to 24 hours ahead.)

3. Cook the pasta in the boiling water until al dente, about 10 minutes. Drain into a colander, rinse under cold water, and drain well.

4. Toss the cooked pasta with the bell pepper, celery, onion, and lobster meat. Drizzle most of the dressing over the pasta and toss until well blended. Season with salt and pepper to taste. If the salad is dry, add the remaining dressing. Refrigerate for at least 1 hour. (Can be prepared up to 12 hours ahead.)

5. To serve, line a platter with lettuce, spoon the salad into the center, and garnish with the tomato, lemon slices, and dill sprigs.

NOTE: *Cook one 1½-pound hard-shell lobster or two 1-pound soft-shells and remove the meat (see chart, page 15) or purchase picked-out meat.*

~~~~~~

BEST LOBSTER MONTHS

Bruce Brown and Tom Markey, who run competing (in a friendly way) lobster pounds in Seabrook Beach, New Hampshire, agree that the best months for lobster are September through December, when the creatures are meatier than the soft-shells that dominate in July and August.

~~~~~~

Salt and freshly ground
black pepper

About 6 lettuce leaves
for lining platter

1 tomato, cut into wedges

4 thin lemon slices

Fresh dill sprigs for garnish

~~~~~~~~~~~~~~~~~~~~~~

4 SERVINGS

LOBSTER POP QUIZ

True or False?

1. *Female lobsters are sweeter and less tough than male lobsters.*

2. *Lobsters are high in cholesterol and fat.*

3. *Maine sells the biggest lobsters.*

4. *Lobsters scream when you cook them.*

5. *The green tomalley is a delicacy.*

Answers

1. *FALSE. Gender has nothing to do with sweetness or tenderness.*

2. *FALSE. Lobster has less of either than skinless chicken.*

3. *FALSE. In order to protect the fishery, Maine law forbids taking lobsters with bodies (excluding tail) more than 5 inches long. The largest recorded lobster was caught off Nova Scotia and was 3½ feet long and weighed more than 44 pounds.*

4. *FALSE. The high-pitched noise you occasionally hear when lobsters hit the boiling water is steam escaping from the shell.*

5. *TRUE AND FALSE. The tomalley is full of wonderful lobster flavor, but it is a filter organ, so eating it in moderation and with discretion is advised.*

CHAPTER THREE

CHOWDERS AND STEWS

Classic Lobster Stew

3 live lobsters (1¼–1½ pounds each)

6 tablespoons butter

¾ cup dry white wine

2 teaspoons paprika

3 cups whole milk

2 cups heavy cream

Salt

Sprinkling of snipped fresh chives (heretical, but nice)

~~~~~~~~~~~~~~~~

4 MAIN COURSE SERVINGS

The simplicity and plainness of this stew is surprising to some (see sidebar, facing page). Traditionally nothing more than lobster, butter, milk and/or cream, and a dash of paprika, lobster stew is something of a cherished heirloom, "built out of subtleties of understanding," according to food writer John Thorne. A kind of alchemy happens when this stew is allowed to ripen, so that each mouthful is fully infused with the essence of lobster. It makes an elegant lunch, or can star as the centerpiece of a summer supper, accompanied, perhaps, by Calico Vinegar Slaw (page 106) and wedges of Best Blueberry Pie (page 116).

1. Bring 1½ inches of salted water to a boil in a large pot. Meanwhile, place the lobsters in the freezer to numb them if you like.

2. Grasp the lobsters around their middle (I wear rubber gloves when handling them) and plunge them headfirst into the boiling water. Cover immediately and return to a boil. Reduce the heat to medium and steam, rearranging once using tongs so they cook evenly, until the lobsters are done (see the chart on page 15). When fully cooked, the lobsters are bright red, and a sharp tug on one of their antennae pulls it out easily. If in doubt, break apart one lobster where the body meets the tail. The meat should be creamy white, with no translucence.

3. Drain, and when cool enough to handle, crack the tails and claws over a bowl, catching and saving as much juice as you can. Pull out the meat, discard the intestinal vein, and chop the meat into 1-inch chunks. Add to the reserved juices. Scoop the green tomalley out of the bodies and reserve a tablespoon or two. (Although the tomalley looks unappetizing at this point, the color will not affect the finished stew; see sidebar, page 56.) Reserve two of the lobster bodies. Split the bodies and remove the head sacs up near the eyes.

4. Melt the butter in a large soup or stew pot. Add the tomalley and simmer for 5 minutes. Add the wine, bring to a boil, and cook over medium-high heat until the wine is reduced by about half, about 5 minutes. Add the lobster meat and saved juices, sprinkle on the paprika, and cook, stirring, for 2 minutes.

5. Slowly add the milk and cream, stirring constantly. Add the reserved split lobster bodies, pushing down to submerge them in the liquid. (They will contribute flavor.) Cool to room temperature and then refrigerate for at least 6 hours or up to 24 hours.

6. Remove and discard the lobster bodies. Reheat the stew over very low heat, stirring often so it does not curdle. Taste for seasoning and add salt if necessary. Ladle into bowls, sprinkle with the chives if desired, and serve.

MISUNDERSTOOD STEW

[Upon tasting her first bowl of lobster stew at Maine's Moody's Diner]

"You'd think it would have thickness, potatoes, or other vegetables. I wasn't disappointed, just surprised. I wonder why it's called a stew."

Twenty-year-old Canadian-born Joanna Repka, quoted in *Joy of Historical Cooking*

Lobster Gazpacho

3 cups roughly torn crustless country bread

2 cups seafood broth or clam juice (see Note)

1 1/2 cups tomato or mixed vegetable juice, plus more if necessary

5 ripe tomatoes (1 3/4– 2 pounds), seeded and roughly chopped (4–5 cups)

1 red bell pepper, seeded and roughly chopped

1 1/2 cups roughly chopped peeled English cucumber

1 cup roughly chopped red onion

1 garlic clove, roughly chopped

1/4 cup fresh basil leaves, plus small sprigs for garnish

1/2 cup extra-virgin olive oil

1/4 cup sherry vinegar

1/2 teaspoon liquid hot pepper sauce, or to taste

Ingredients continue opposite

Based on an Andalusian classic, this gazpacho is an adaptation of a recipe in Jasper White's *Lobster at Home*. Lobster adds a decidedly delicious dimension, and seafood broth helps to further punch up the lobster flavor. Serve this refreshing soup/salad on a sultry summer day.

1. Combine the bread, broth, tomato juice, tomatoes, bell pepper, cucumber, onion, garlic, and basil leaves in a large bowl. Let stand until the bread softens, at least 10 minutes.

2. Process the bread mixture in batches in a blender or food processor to make a fairly smooth purée. With the last batch in the machine, and with the motor running, add the olive oil and vinegar in a stream. Combine all the batches in a large bowl, season with hot pepper sauce and salt and pepper to taste, and refrigerate for at least 2 hours, until thoroughly chilled. If the soup is too thick, thin with additional tomato juice. (Can be made a day ahead.)

3. Ladle the soup into bowls and float the lobster medallions on top. Garnish with basil sprigs and serve.

Salt and freshly
ground black pepper

5 ounces cooked lobster
tails, cut into medallions
(about 1 cup) (see Note)

～～～～～～～

4 LIGHT MAIN
COURSE SERVINGS;
6 STARTER SERVINGS

～～～～～～～

LOBSTER HUES

Most live lobsters are a mottled blackish-greenish color, but occasionally lobsters of another color are caught. The occasional blue lobster is pulled up in a trap and an extremely rare yellow lobster (one in every 30 million, it's estimated) was caught by a Narragansett Bay, Rhode Island, fisherman in 2010.

～～～～～～～

NOTES:

1. Seafood broth or stock can often be found in supermarkets near the chicken and beef broth. Bottled clam juice is shelved with the canned seafood. If the clam juice is salty, dilute with water. A recipe for Quick Lobster Broth is found on page 15.

2. Cook one 1½-pound hard-shell lobster and use the tail meat (see chart, page 15) or buy picked-out tail meat or a rock lobster tail.

A Not-Too-Rich Lobster Bisque

6 tablespoons butter

1 medium-large
onion, chopped

1 carrot, finely chopped

1 large garlic clove,
finely chopped

2 medium-large
plum tomatoes, seeded
and chopped

1 cup dry white wine

1 bay leaf

1 tablespoon chopped
fresh thyme

4 cups seafood broth or
clam juice (see Note)

1½ cups chopped
cooked lobster meat
(8 ounces) (see Note)

2 lobster bodies,
if available

1 cup heavy cream

Ingredients continue opposite

I've eaten my share of overly rich and overly thickened bisques, so I've developed one here that is creamy and full of flavor but not too filling. If you have lobster bodies, steeping them in the hot soup contributes additional deep lobster flavor, but the bisque is quite delicious made with lobster meat alone.

1. Melt the butter in a large soup pot. Add the onion, carrot, and garlic, and cook over medium-low heat until the carrot is softened, about 15 minutes.

2. Add the tomatoes, wine, bay leaf, and thyme, bring to a boil, and boil briskly until the liquid is reduced by about half, 3 to 5 minutes. Add the broth and cook, uncovered, over medium heat until slightly reduced, about 5 minutes. Add the lobster meat and simmer for 2 minutes. (If you have lobster bodies, split them, remove the head sacs up near the eyes, add the lobsters to the hot liquid, cover the pot, and set aside for 1 hour at room temperature. Even better, refrigerate overnight, and then remove the bodies and proceed with the recipe.)

3. Remove the bay leaf and purée the soup in batches in a blender until smooth (see Note). Stir in the cream and sherry and season with salt and pepper to taste. (Can be made a day ahead and refrigerated, or

frozen.) Reheat the bisque gently, ladle into bowls, sprinkle with paprika, and serve.

NOTES:

1. Seafood broth or stock can often be found in supermarkets near the chicken and beef broth. Bottled clam juice is shelved with the canned seafood. If the clam juice is salty, dilute with water. A recipe for Quick Lobster Broth is found on page 15.

2. Cook one 1½-pound hard-shell lobster or two 1-pound soft-shells and remove the meat (see chart, page 15) or buy picked-out meat.

3. This type of mixture with a fairly large quantity of liquid does not purée well in a food processor. Use a blender or immersion blender or pass through a food mill.

3 tablespoons medium-dry sherry

Salt and freshly ground black pepper

Paprika

MAKES 5–6 CUPS
(5–6 FIRST COURSE
SERVINGS; 4 MAIN COURSE
LUNCHEON SERVINGS)

RO-DYE-LAN' SPEAK

Rhode Islanders have their own unique accent and vocabulary. Don Bousquet, Rhode Island humorist, might ask, "Jeetya [did you eat your] lobstah chowdah yet?"

THE GRANT FAMILY, FISHERMEN

Bill Grant of Carter Point, Sedgwick, Maine, goes fishing every summer. One early summer morning, his large, sturdy lobster boat, the Sharlene IV, carries Bill, his sternman (today it happens to be Patrick, Bill's son), and your author out of the harbor through the fog, heading east to Jericho Bay for a day of lobstering. Conversation is difficult over the thrum of the diesel engines, so I stand aside, trying just to stay out of the way and watch, at first. Within a few minutes, Bill is leaning out to snag the first red and white buoy with his gaff, lifting the line over the snatch block, steering with one hand, operating the pot hauler (winch) engine with the other, kicking the potentially dangerous line out of the way on the deck as it reels in, brushing away hunks of potentially dangerous slippery seaweed, until the 30- to 40-pound steel wire trap is dangling over the deck. With a muscle-straining heave, Bill drags it up onto the gunwales of the boat, and then with precise, concentrated movements, orchestrated without conversation, Bill flips up the top of the trap, Patrick empties the remnants of the bait bag into the sea and ties a new one on, Bill removes the lobsters and releases the line from the pot hauler, Patrick shoves the pot back in the water, and Bill shifts the engine back into gear. As Bill steers toward the next pot, Patrick measures the lobsters, throwing any "shorts" back overboard, attaches heavy rubber bands around the two large claws of the keepers, and then begins refilling nylon bait bags with more salted herring. He must be ready in less than a minute or so to haul the next trap.

And so it goes all morning, as the fog burns off, the sun moves up in a cloudless blue sky over a glassy sea, and gulls wheel and cry over the boat. By noon, after a five-minute break for lunch, they've hauled more than 300 traps, and I'm tired and sore just watching. Finally, when we hit a string of particularly full traps, my offer to be put to work is accepted. Wearing rubber gloves, I help with stuffing bait bags and handing Patrick supplies for banding. The sun begins its downward course, the breeze freshens, and we're now in the far easternmost edge of the bay, continuing to move systematically through fields of buoys, still snagging lines, hauling traps, shoving them back, and packing seawater-filled barrels and slatted boxes brimfull of beautiful shiny-black Homarus americanus.

In mid-afternoon, they shove the last pot overboard. As Bill steers homeward through the bay, Patrick scrubs the boat down and organizes the catch while I sit numbly in a corner, almost too tired to appreciate the beauty of the fir-tipped islands, pink granite ledges, and harbor seals. This was an idyllic weather day, all conditions perfect. How do these fishermen do it day after day, I wonder, when the boat is pitching in 10- to 15-foot waves, rain squalls slamming their faces, clammy fog obscuring visibility, and the cold numbing their fingers and feet? I emerge out the other end of this day with heightened respect for the people who are engaged in this arduous, yet often deeply rewarding, work.

"This was a good day, one of our best days yet this summer," Bill says. Countless hundreds of traps hauled, and over 500 lobsters to take to market at the wholesaler in Deer Isle. "But our best day ever was a couple of years ago, when my sister Sharlene was working with us," says Patrick. "That day the three of us took almost 800 lobsters." "And Sharlene banded every single one of them," Bill smiles, with just a modest Yankee hint of fraternal pride.

Rhode Island Red Lobster Stew

5 tablespoons plus
2 teaspoons olive oil

2 large garlic cloves,
thinly sliced

2 jalapeño peppers, minced,
including seeds (see Note)

2 medium leeks, trimmed
and sliced crosswise, white
and light green parts only

1 large onion, chopped

1 tablespoon finely
chopped fresh rosemary,
plus sprigs for garnish

2 cups dry white wine

1 cup water

1 (28-ounce) can
imported plum tomatoes
with juice (see Note)

1 bay leaf

1 sweet potato (about
10 ounces), peeled and
cubed (2½ cups)

Ingredients continue opposite

This Mediterranean-inspired lobster stew is an adaptation of one of George Germon and Johanne Killeen's recipes published in the *New York Times*. The duo are chef/owners of Providence, Rhode Island's renowned Al Forno, and are famous for their gutsy yet sophisticated cooking. Note that the sliced garlic and hot pepper are cooked in the olive oil until blackened, which is counter to most received wisdom, but the char adds incredible depth of flavor to the stew. Crusty Portuguese bread, a mesclun salad, and Lemon-Buttermilk Sponge Tart (page 128) would complete the meal beautifully.

1. Heat the 5 tablespoons oil in a very large soup pot. Add the garlic and jalapeños and cook over medium-high heat until the jalapeños are almost black, 3 to 4 minutes. Add the leeks, onion, and chopped rosemary, and cook over medium heat, stirring occasionally, until the vegetables are beginning to soften, about 8 minutes. Add the wine, water, tomatoes, and bay leaf. Use kitchen scissors to cut the tomatoes into smaller chunks or break them up with the side of a spoon. Bring to a boil, reduce the heat to medium-low, and simmer, uncovered, until reduced and thickened, about 30 minutes. Add the sweet potato and cook, covered, for 10 minutes.

2. Follow the directions for splitting live lobsters on page 16. Remove the rubber bands, crack the claws if the lobsters are hard-shells, and leave some of the tomalley in the bodies for flavor if desired. Add

the lobster halves (including the bodies, which contribute flavor) to the stew, cover, and bring to a boil. Reduce the heat to medium-low and cook until the lobster shells are red and the meat is opaque, 10 to 15 minutes. Using tongs, remove the lobster to a large bowl, scraping off as much sauce as possible.

3 When the lobster is cool enough to handle, crack the claws and pick out the meat. Cut the tail meat into bite-size pieces, but leave the claws intact and slice them lengthwise to preserve their shape if possible. Return any lobster juices to the pot and season with salt and pepper to taste. (Can be made up to a day ahead. Refrigerate the stew base and lobster meat separately.)

4 If you have refrigerated the stew, reheat the base over medium heat. It should be quite thick; reduce it if it's too thin; add water if it's too thick. Toss the lobster meat in a large skillet over medium-high heat with the 2 teaspoons oil until heated through.

5 To serve, spoon the vegetable stew mixture into shallow soup bowls and arrange the lobster meat on top. Garnish with rosemary sprigs and top with a lemon wedge for squeezing.

NOTES:

1. *The long cooking tames the peppers' heat, but if you want a less spicy result, use just one jalapeño.*

2. *San Marzano tomatoes are a good choice.*

4 live lobsters, about 1¼ pounds each, rinsed

Salt and freshly ground black pepper

Lemon wedges for garnish

4 SERVINGS

HOW THE LOBSTER GOT ITS SHELL

"It is apparent to serious shellfish eaters that in the great evolutionary scheme of things crustaceans developed shells to protect them from knives and forks."

Calvin Trillin,
Alice, Let's Eat

Lobster and Sweet Corn Chowder

This is an utterly delicious and gorgeous-to-look-at chowder, with its nuggets of yellow corn, pink-tinged lobster meat, and flecks of green thyme, spangled on top with pools of melted butter. It's some work to make, so when I go to the effort I make this chowder the star as a main course and serve it with Focaccia Garlic Toasts (page 114) and a platter of sliced tomatoes and basil dribbled with good olive oil. Either Strawberry Shortcake (page 124) or Cranberry-Orange Upside-Down Cake (page 122) would be an ideal finish.

1. Bring 7 cups of water to a boil in a large soup pot and add the 1 teaspoon salt.

2. Grasp the lobsters around their middle (I wear rubber gloves when handling them) and plunge them headfirst into the boiling water. Cover immediately and return to a boil. Cook, covered, until the lobsters are bright red and fully cooked, about 10 minutes per pound (see the chart on page 15). Use tongs to remove the lobsters to a bowl, leaving the cooking liquid in the pot. Separate and set aside the claws and tails. Rinse most of the tomalley from the bodies, split them, remove the head sacs up near the eyes, and return the split bodies to the pot.

3. Return the liquid to a boil, and then reduce the heat to low and simmer for 15 minutes. Strain the broth

Recipe continues on next page

1 teaspoon salt,
plus more if needed

4 live lobsters
(1¼–1½ pounds each),
rinsed (see Note)

¼ pound bacon, chopped

1 large onion, chopped

1 large celery stalk,
thinly sliced

2 tablespoons all-purpose flour

½ cup dry white wine

4 medium all-purpose
potatoes, peeled and diced
(about 4 cups)

4 ears corn, kernels
cut from the cob,
or 2 cups frozen kernels

2 tablespoons
chopped fresh thyme

2 cups heavy cream

¼ teaspoon cayenne pepper

Freshly ground black pepper

6 tablespoons butter

6 MAIN COURSE SERVINGS

"It is the green stuff in the central core of the lobster which is the quintessence of the creature and the nearest we mortals can come to the ambrosia of the Greek gods. People have been known to shy away from this substance and put it gingerly to one side.... Multiply all the taste in the lobster by ten, by twenty, and you have this emerald delicacy which tops all flavors of the world."

Robert P. Tristram Coffin,
Mainstays of Maine

through a medium-mesh strainer into a large bowl. You should have about 5 cups of broth.

4. Meanwhile, pick out the lobster claw and tail meat, chop it into bite-size pieces, and refrigerate. (Can be done up to 24 hours ahead.)

5. Cook the bacon in a large soup pot over medium-low heat until the fat is rendered and the bacon is crisp, about 15 minutes. Remove the bacon with a slotted spoon, drain on paper towels, and reserve. Add the onion and celery to the fat in the pot and cook over medium-high heat until softened, about 5 minutes. Add the flour and cook, stirring, for 1 minute. Add the wine and the 5 cups lobster broth, and bring to a boil, stirring. Add the potatoes, corn, and thyme, and return to a boil. Reduce the heat to low and simmer, covered, until the potatoes are almost tender, about 15 minutes.

6. Add the lobster meat, cream, and cayenne, and simmer uncovered for 5 minutes. Taste and season with salt and pepper as necessary. Cut the butter into chunks and add to the chowder to melt. You can serve immediately, but the chowder will be even more flavorful if you refrigerate it overnight.

7. Reheat the reserved bacon bits in the microwave. Ladle the chowder into soup bowls, sprinkle with the bacon, and serve.

NOTE: *You can also use 1 pound (about 3 cups) chopped picked-out lobster meat and 5 cups seafood broth, clam juice, or a combination of clam juice and water. Seafood broth or stock can often be found in supermarkets near the chicken and beef broth. Bottled clam juice is shelved with the canned seafood. If the clam juice is salty, dilute with water.*

CHAPTER FOUR

MAINS

Plain Steamed or Boiled Lobster

The simplest — and some would argue, the best — way to prepare lobsters is to steam or boil the "bugs" and serve them up with nothing more than melted butter spiked with a little vinegar or lemon juice. I steam soft-shells (also called new-shells or shedders) and I boil hard-shell lobsters. (See note at end of recipe.) To make this a classic shore dinner, serve steamed mussels or clams as an appetizer and add corn on the cob, Creamy Coleslaw (page 104) or Tomato, Watermelon, and Feta Salad (page 110), and Focaccia Garlic Toasts (page 114) to the menu. I like to let the lobsters star, so I always serve the vegetables as a separate course after the lobsters. (Plus lobster plates can get pretty messy...) Dessert needs to be Best Blueberry Pie (page 116).

1. Fill a large (4- to 5-gallon) kettle or two smaller pots with about 1½ inches of water. Add about 1 tablespoon salt and bring to a boil. Meanwhile, place the lobsters in the freezer to numb them, if you like.

2. Grasp the lobsters around their middle (I wear rubber gloves when handling them) and plunge them headfirst into the boiling water. Cover immediately and return to a boil. Reduce the heat to medium and steam, rearranging once using tongs so they cook evenly, until the lobsters are done (see the

Recipe continues on next page

Salt

4 live soft-shell lobsters, at least 1¼ pounds each (see Note)

½ cup (1 stick) butter, melted (see Note)

1–2 tablespoons cider vinegar, white wine vinegar, and/or lemon juice

4 SERVINGS

MOLT MUCH?

In Richard King's book, Lobster, the self-proclaimed "lobsterologist" estimates that by the time we eat a one-and-a-quarter-pound male lobster it is probably seven or eight years old and has molted at least 25 times.

Jasper White, famed chef and lobster authority, says, "A lobster roll is humble, but don't be fooled by the garnish of pickles and potato chips. This dish is like a millionaire driving an old Chevy — understated, but still rich — typical of the New England culture."

chart on page 15). When fully cooked, the lobsters are bright red, and a sharp tug on one of their antennae pulls it out easily. If in doubt, break apart one lobster where the body meets the tail. The meat should be creamy white, with no translucence.

3 Remove the lobsters with tongs and transfer to a colander in the sink. Place on plates and serve as is, or, if desired, perform either of the following refinements: Use the tip of a small knife to punch a hole between the lobsters' eyes and hold over the sink to drain off excess liquid. Use a large knife to split the lobsters down through the underside of the tails and drain again.

4 Divide the melted butter into small bowls and add vinegar or lemon juice (your choice, they serve the same function) to one or two of the bowls so that guests have a choice between the richness of plain butter and the brighter flavor of vinegar or lemon butter.

NOTES:

1. To cook hard-shells, bring a large pot of water to a boil and add about 2 tablespoons salt. Plunge the lobsters head-first into the water, cover, return to a boil, and cook as above for about 15 minutes (see chart, page 15).

2. Some older recipes call for drawn butter — melted butter with the milk solids at the bottom discarded — but I think pouring off the milk solids is an unnecessary step.

A BACKYARD CLAMBAKE

⚓ *A simplified, scaled-down backyard or beach version of a clambake involves a fraction of the work yet still produces one of the most extravagant and downright delicious meals of summer. (See page 65 for tips on doing a traditional lobster bake.) I use this method when cooking lobsters for more than about six people.*

⚓ *Set a large pot (I use a turkey fryer) on a tripod over a propane burner or over a wood fire on a beach or in a safe backyard spot.*

⚓ *Boil or steam lobsters, clams or mussels, and corn. Serve on paper plates with little cups of melted butter and lemon wedges. Provide lobster bibs and paper towels.*

⚓ *Add other items to the menu such as New Potato Salad with Egg and Pickle (page 108) or Creamy Coleslaw (page 104), Focaccia Garlic Toasts (page 114), and Best Blueberry Pie (page 116) for dessert.*

Grilled Lobster
with Basil-Lime Butter

Lobster is an excellent candidate for grilling, either split raw, or parboiled. (Both instructions follow. If you don't mind splitting them live, it saves a step.) The shells cradle the meat, creating a natural and spectacular-looking cooking and serving container, while at the same time offering protection from the intensity of the heat. The sweet lobster flesh is enhanced by the smoky grill flavor, and the red shells develop an attractive black char here and there. Good go-withs are Grilled Chili-Lime Corn on the Cob (page 113), grilled country bread, and Rustic Summer Fruit Tart (page 119).

1. Melt the butter in a small saucepan. Stir in the basil, lime zest and juice, salt, and cayenne.

2. Parboil the lobsters, split them, and prepare for further cooking (see instructions on page 17), or split the lobsters live (see page 16). Parboiled lobsters can be refrigerated for up to 4 hours; split live lobsters should be cooked within about 1 hour.

3. Build a moderately hot charcoal fire or preheat a gas grill to medium-high.

4. Rub the lobster shells with the oil. Place the lobsters on the grill cut sides up, brush the meat with the butter mixture, and sprinkle with paprika. Close the grill lid or place a shallow metal roasting pan

Recipe continues on next page

4 tablespoons butter

3 tablespoons slivered fresh basil

1 1/2 teaspoons grated lime zest

1 tablespoon lime juice

1/2 teaspoon salt

1/4 teaspoon cayenne pepper, or to taste

2 large live lobsters (1 3/4-2 pounds) or 4 smaller lobsters

2 tablespoons vegetable oil

Paprika

Lime wedges for garnish

4 SERVINGS

over the lobsters. Cook, without turning, brushing once or twice with more flavored butter, until the meat is a creamy opaque white but still juicy, 10 to 15 minutes if starting them raw, 8 to 10 minutes if parboiled. (Smaller lobsters will take less time to cook.)

5 Transfer the lobster to a platter or serving plates, brush with more of the butter, and serve with lime wedges.

iLOBSTER

Feeling a bit uncertain about your lobster-cracking skills? Step-by-step instructions are now just a click away by downloading an iPhone app with the tag line "Click. Crack. Eat." The application also features a lobster restaurant locator and information on where to order live lobsters from local dealers. See it at www.ilobsterapp.com.

A REAL NICE CLAMBAKE

This ancient, primal lobster cooking method is called a lobster bake in Maine and a clambake along the rest of the Atlantic coast. The tradition is inherited directly from the Native Americans, who cooked all their food this way in their summer encampments up and down the New England coastline. The basic method starts with digging a deep pit in the sand and lining it with rocks upon which is built a driftwood or hardwood fire. When the fire burns down, the coals are raked away and wet rockweed seaweed, which is laden with tiny sacs full of salt water, is layered over the white-hot rocks. The food goes on over the seaweed and a heavy canvas tarp is spread over it all to seal in the heat. As the rockweed heats and releases water vapor, this salty steam cooks the food. When the tarp is lifted, the heavenly ocean-sweet, smoky aroma of steamed seafood perfumes the sea air.

Traditional clambake elements include lobsters, clams, corn, pota-toes, and — anywhere near Rhode Island, with its large Portuguese popu-lation — spicy smoked sausage. Other ingredients vary from one locale to the next. Mussels, chicken, onions, sweet potatoes, crabs, whole fish, and eggs are sometimes added.

Constructing a genuine pit-in-the-sand clambake on a beach takes superb organizational skill and is at least an all-day affair. You need a group of hard-working family or friends — or, for a community fundraiser, a diligent committee. Serving as the "bakemaster" is an honored posi-tion that must be earned by serving years of apprenticeship as a bake-master's helper.

Baked Stuffed Spectacular

4 live lobsters
(1¼–1½ pounds each)

½ cup (1 stick) butter

¾ cup chopped onion

About 1 tablespoon
tomalley (optional)

About 1 tablespoon
lobster roe (optional)

1 cup dry breadcrumbs
or panko crumbs

2 tablespoons
medium-dry sherry

¼ cup chopped fresh
flat-leaf parsley

Salt and freshly
ground black pepper

Lemon wedges for garnish

~~~~~~~~~~~~~~~~~

4 SERVINGS

You might think of baked stuffed lobster as the ultimate special-occasion-at-a-restaurant treat, but, in fact, it's not all that hard to do at home. It is a spectacular dish — both to look at and to eat. To ready for stuffing and baking you can split the live lobsters or parboil them first. This main course calls for simple accompaniments such as a lightly dressed green salad and good crusty bread, but it would be nice to start the meal with a Composed Salad of Tomatoes, Blueberries, and Goat Cheese (page 111). Chocolate Bread and Butter Pudding with Rum Custard Sauce (page 134) is a fitting finale.

1. Parboil the lobsters, split them, and prepare for further cooking (see instructions on page 17), or split the lobsters live (see page 16). Scoop out the tomalley and roe to use in the stuffing if desired. Parboiled lobsters can be refrigerated for up to 4 hours; split live lobsters should be cooked within about 1 hour.

2. Melt 4 tablespoons of the butter in a large skillet. Add the onion and tomalley and roe, if desired, and cook over medium heat until the onion softens, about 5 minutes. Add the breadcrumbs and cook, stirring frequently, until lightly toasted and golden, 3 to 4 minutes. Stir in the sherry and parsley, and season with ¼ teaspoon salt and ⅛ teaspoon pepper. (Crumbs can be made several hours ahead and refrigerated. If you make the stuffing before you remove the lobster

tomalley and roe, simmer them in water for a few minutes and add to the prepared stuffing.)

3. Preheat the oven to 450 degrees.

4. Melt the remaining 4 tablespoons butter. Brush butter over the cut sides of the lobsters and sprinkle lightly with salt and pepper. Sprinkle the crumbs evenly over the body cavities and tail meat. Drizzle with any remaining melted butter.

5. Bake, uncovered, for 15 to 20 minutes, until the tail meat is opaque and the crumbs are deep golden brown. Serve with lemon wedges.

COOL TOOLS

Hard-shell lobsters are too … hard … to crack with your hands. The shells need to be broken with a hammer or cracked with a nutcracker to get at the meat. A nut pick or similar tool (a chopstick works well) can help push the meat out of the claws. Plastic bibs are fun as well as useful, and a debris bowl for shells is a necessity on the table.

Lobster Cakes
on Greens Vinaigrette

1 egg

½ cup mayonnaise

2 teaspoons lemon zest

2 tablespoons lemon juice

¼ cup finely chopped fresh chives or scallions

¼ teaspoons freshly ground black pepper

1½ cups fresh breadcrumbs or panko crumbs

3 cups cooked lobster meat, chopped into ½-inch chunks (1 pound) (see Note)

3 tablespoons light olive oil or vegetable oil

4 handfuls mixed mesclun greens

About ¼ cup homemade vinaigrette (such as Simple Vinaigrette, page 105) or good quality bottled vinaigrette

Lemon wedges for garnish

~~~~~~~~~~~~~~~~

4 SERVINGS

I've taken my formula for crab cakes and adapted it to lobster meat, with delicious results. The cakes are served on a bed of mesclun dressed with vinaigrette, which nicely balances the richness of the lobster. Serve with steamed asparagus or Grilled Chili-Lime Corn on the Cob (page 113). Lemon-Buttermilk Sponge Tart (page 128) would complete the meal in fine fashion.

1. Lightly beat the egg in a large bowl. Whisk in the mayonnaise, lemon zest and juice, chives, and pepper, and then stir in the crumbs. Add the lobster meat and stir gently but thoroughly to combine. Shape the mixture into 8 patties about ½ inch thick and place on a waxed paper–lined baking sheet. Refrigerate, covered, for at least 30 minutes or up to 6 hours, until the cakes are firm.

2. Heat the oil in two large skillets. Cook the lobster cakes over medium heat, uncovered, until nicely browned, 3 to 5 minutes. Turn, cover the pans, reduce the heat to medium-low, and cook until the undersides are golden and the cakes are hot in the center, about 3 minutes.

3. Mound the greens on four plates or a serving platter and drizzle lightly with the vinaigrette. Serve the

lobster cakes on top of the greens and garnish with lemon wedges.

NOTE: *Cook three 1¼-pound hard-shell lobsters or four 1-pound soft-shells and remove the meat (see chart, page 15) or buy picked-out meat.*

Softly Scrambled Eggs
with Lobster

8 eggs

1/4 cup cream cheese, softened

3 tablespoons shredded medium-sharp cheddar cheese

2 tablespoons finely chopped red bell pepper

2 tablespoons thinly sliced scallions, plus 1 tablespoon finely chopped green parts for garnish

3/4 teaspoon salt

1/4 teaspoon freshly ground black pepper

1 cup chopped cooked lobster meat (5 ounces) (see Note)

3 tablespoons butter

~~~~~~~~~~~~~~~~

3-4 SERVINGS

This beautifully rich lobster scrambled egg recipe is an adaptation of a dish served at the Island Inn on Maine's Monhegan Island. If you have leftover lobster dipping butter, use it in the pan. For brunch, accompany with toasted English muffins and a selection of local jams and jellies. If serving as a light supper, a simple green salad and grilled focaccia would round things out nicely.

1. Whisk the eggs in a large bowl. Break the cream cheese into rough ½-inch chunks (so it will incorporate) and add it to the eggs along with the cheddar, bell pepper, sliced scallions, salt, and pepper. Stir in the lobster.

2. Melt the butter in a large skillet, preferably nonstick. Add the egg mixture and cook over low heat, stirring almost constantly with a wooden spatula, until the eggs are softly scrambled or reach the desired consistency. Spoon onto plates, sprinkle with scallion greens, and serve.

NOTE: *Use leftover meat or cook one 1¼-pound hard-shell lobster or two 1-pound soft-shells and remove the meat (see chart, page 15) or buy picked-out meat.*

Lobster Pasta
with Tomato-Caper Cream Sauce

This recipe is adapted from a similar one in the first Silver Palate cookbook, a book full of wonderfully flavorful dishes. Tomatoes, cream, and capers blend to make a sauce that perfectly complements the lobster. Any type of strand pasta is fine, but I like bucatini — a fatter, chewier, hollow spaghetti — for this dish. An arugula salad and crusty seeded Italian bread are good accompaniments, and Lemon Blueberry Mousse (page 126) is the perfect finish.

1. Heat the oil in a large deep skillet. Add the garlic and cook over medium heat for 2 minutes. Add the tomatoes, wine, and ½ teaspoon salt, and bring to a boil. Reduce the heat to low and simmer, covered, for 15 minutes.

2. Add the cream, tarragon, and cayenne, and return to a boil. Reduce the heat to medium and cook, uncovered, until slightly reduced and thickened, about 5 minutes. Stir in the lobster meat and remove from the heat. (Can be made up to a day ahead and refrigerated.)

3. Bring a large pot of salted water to a boil and cook the pasta until al dente, about 10 minutes.

4. Meanwhile, if necessary, reheat the sauce over low heat.

Recipe continues on next page

3 tablespoons olive oil

3 garlic cloves, minced

2 (28-ounce) cans imported plum tomatoes, drained and chopped (see Note)

½ cup white wine

Salt

1 cup heavy cream

2 tablespoons chopped fresh tarragon

¼ teaspoon cayenne pepper

3 cups diced cooked lobster meat (1 pound) (see Note)

1 pound bucatini or other strand pasta

½ cup thinly sliced scallions, white and green parts

3 tablespoons drained capers

Freshly ground black pepper

4–5 SERVINGS

5 In a large serving bowl, toss the pasta with the sauce, scallions, and capers. Season with additional salt and pepper to taste, and serve.

NOTES:

1. Use top-quality Italian plum tomatoes such as San Marzano, which are now readily available in supermarkets.

2. Cook three 1¼-pound hard-shell lobsters or four 1-pound soft-shells and remove the meat (see chart, page 15) or buy picked-out meat.

GREENLAW ON LOBSTER

"Many things taste like chicken but nothing tastes like lobster."

LOBSTER APPLAUSE

"I loved the sound of the lobsters' shells' muffled applause as they clapped against themselves and one another in the end of a trap fresh from the water. A full trap sounded like a standing ovation."

Linda Greenlaw, *The Lobster Chronicles*

Lobster Mac and Cheese

Mac and Cheese

3 tablespoons butter

1/3 cup minced onion

1 small garlic clove, minced

1/4 cup all-purpose flour

1 1/2 cups whole milk

1 cup seafood broth
or clam juice (see Note)

6 ounces Gruyère cheese,
shredded (1 1/2 cups)

6 ounces sharp cheddar
cheese, shredded (1 1/2 cups)

1/4 teaspoon freshly
ground black pepper

1/8 teaspoon cayenne pepper

1/8 teaspoon grated nutmeg

Salt

8 ounces cavatappi or elbow
macaroni (see Note)

2 1/4 cups chopped
cooked lobster meat
(12 ounces) (see Note)

Ingredients continue opposite

Rich? Yes indeed – some could say even sinfully so – but guaranteed to be one of the best renditions of comfort food you've ever tasted. Ina Garten popularized the concept of lobster macaroni and cheese and now it pops up on high-end menus across the country. This recipe uses Ina's as a starting point, but I've tweaked it to my taste. Serve a tomato and red onion salad on the side and a lemon dessert such as Lemon-Buttermilk Sponge Tart (page 128).

1. Bring a large pot of salted water to a boil for the pasta.

2. Melt the butter in a medium-large saucepan, add the onion, and cook over medium heat until softened, about 5 minutes. Add the garlic and cook for 1 minute. Sprinkle on the flour, raise the heat to medium-high, and cook, stirring, for 2 minutes. Gradually whisk in the milk and broth and bring to a boil. Cook, whisking, until the sauce is bubbly and thickened, about 2 minutes. Remove from the heat and add the Gruyère and cheddar by handfuls, stirring until melted. Whisk in the black pepper, cayenne, nutmeg, and 3/4 teaspoon salt.

3. Cook the pasta in the boiling water until al dente, 8 to 10 minutes. Drain the pasta and toss with the sauce and lobster meat. Taste for salt, adding more if necessary. Scrape the mixture into a buttered 2-quart baking dish.

4. To make the topping, melt the butter in a small skillet. Add the crumbs and cook over medium heat, stirring

frequently, until pale golden, 2 to 3 minutes. Remove from the heat and stir in the cheese. Sprinkle evenly over the pasta.

5. If serving later, cover the baking dish with foil and refrigerate for up to 6 hours, or freeze. (If frozen, thaw before baking.) Bake the foil-covered casserole in a preheated 350-degree oven for 20 minutes, then uncover and bake for about 40 minutes, until the cheese and crumbs are lightly browned and the sauce is bubbly.

6. If serving immediately, preheat the oven to 375 degrees. Bake the casserole uncovered until the sauce is bubbly around the edges and the crumbs are lightly browned, 20 to 25 minutes.

NOTES:

1. Seafood broth or stock can often be found in supermarkets near the chicken and beef broth. Bottled clam juice is shelved with the canned seafood. If the clam juice is salty, dilute with water. A recipe for Quick Lobster Broth is found on page 15.

2. Cavatappi is a double spiral elbow pasta, usually with lines or grooves on the outside surface. It is also known as cellentani or trivella. If you can't find it, old-fashioned elbow macaroni is fine.

3. Cook two 1½-pound hard-shell lobsters or three 1-pound soft shells and remove the meat (see chart, page 15) or buy picked-out meat.

Topping

2 tablespoons butter

½ cup fresh breadcrumbs or panko crumbs

1 ounce sharp cheddar cheese, shredded (¼ cup)

4-6 SERVINGS

LOBSTER PARAPHERNALIA

The gift shop at the Lobster Claw restaurant in Orleans on Cape Cod carries more than 250 lobster-related items on its shelves.

Roasted Tomatoes

12 plum tomatoes
(about 1½ pounds)

1–2 tablespoons olive oil

Salt and freshly ground
black pepper

~~~~~~~~~~~~~~~~~~

Risotto

3 tablespoons butter

1 medium onion, chopped

2 garlic cloves,
finely chopped

1 cup Arborio rice

1 cup fresh corn kernels
(from 2 ears of corn)

1 cup white wine

4 cups seafood broth or
clam juice (see Note)

1½ cups roughly chopped
cooked lobster meat
(8 ounces) (see Note)

Ingredients continue opposite

Lobster and Corn Risotto
with Roasted Tomatoes

I make this at the height of summer when corn and tomatoes are fresh and local. Roasting the tomatoes concentrates flavor and brings out their natural sweetness — a good fit for lobster, the starring ingredient. Add a salad of light lettuces and finish with Rustic Summer Fruit Tart (page 119) for a lovely seasonal dinner.

1. To make the tomatoes, preheat the oven to 350 degrees.

2. Core the tomatoes, cut them into quarters, and spread them on a rimmed baking sheet. Drizzle the tomatoes with the oil and sprinkle with salt and pepper. Roast, stirring once or twice, until the tomatoes soften, give up their juice, and begin to caramelize, about 1½ hours. Scrape into a container and refrigerate. (Can be made up to 3 days ahead. Return to room temperature before using.)

3. To make the risotto, melt the butter in a large saucepan. Add the onion and cook over medium-high heat until softened, about 5 minutes. Add the garlic and cook for 1 minute. Add the rice and cook, stirring, until the grains are coated with butter and slightly translucent, about 2 minutes. Add the corn and wine, bring to a boil, and cook until most of the liquid evaporates, about 2 minutes.

4. Meanwhile, heat the broth in a saucepan. Pour about one-third of the hot liquid over the rice and cook over medium heat, at a barely bubbling simmer, stirring almost constantly, until the liquid is absorbed, about 5 minutes. Repeat with another third of the broth and cook for 5 minutes. Repeat with the last third of the broth, cooking until the rice is almost tender.

5. Add the lobster, torn basil, and Parmesan, and cook, stirring, until the rice is tender but still slightly firm to the bite, about 3 minutes. Season with the salt and pepper. Scatter the roasted tomatoes over the top of the risotto.

6. Serve directly from the pot, garnished with basil.

NOTES:

1. Seafood broth or stock can often be found in supermarkets near the chicken and beef broth. Bottled clam juice is shelved with the canned seafood. If the clam juice is salty, dilute with water. A recipe for Quick Lobster Broth is found on page 15.

2. Cook one 1½-pound hard-shell lobster or two 1-pound soft-shells and remove the meat (see chart, page 15) or buy picked-out meat.

⅓ cup torn fresh basil leaves, plus leaves for garnish

¼ cup grated Parmesan cheese

¾ teaspoon salt

¼ teaspoon freshly ground black pepper

4 SERVINGS

FISHERMEN'S PERFUME

"His clothes always smelled of gasoline and fish."

Leo Connellan,
The Maine Poems

Lobster and Smoked Ham
on Cheese Grits

Lobster and Ham

2 tablespoons olive oil

1½ cups finely diced
tasso or smoked ham
(about 6 ounces) (see Note)

2 tablespoons butter

2 tablespoons
all-purpose flour

1½ cups seafood broth or
clam juice (see Note)

1 cup finely diced seeded
tomatoes

½ cup thinly sliced scallions,
white and green parts

3 cups roughly chopped
cooked lobster meat
(1 pound) (see Note)

⅓ cup chopped fresh
flat-leaf parsley

2 tablespoons lemon juice

Salt and freshly ground
black pepper

~~~~~~~~~~~~~~~~~

Ingredients continue opposite

Shrimp 'n' grits is a wonderful southern specialty, and now that grits are readily available all around the country I thought it would be nice to have a lobster version, which is, in fact, perfectly scrumptious. Northerners never have much bought into the grits-for-breakfast concept but we do seem to like them a lot for supper — especially when enriched with sharp cheddar cheese. Pass a bottle of hot sauce so that people can add heat to their own taste. A salad of crisp bitter greens or Calico Vinegar Slaw (page 106) would be a nice go-with, and Cranberry-Orange Upside-Down Cake (page 122) would end the meal in splendid fashion.

1. Heat the oil in a large deep skillet or saucepan. Add the tasso and cook over medium-low heat until it is tinged with brown, about 8 minutes. Remove the tasso with a slotted spoon, leaving the drippings in the pan.

2. Add the butter to the pan drippings, sprinkle on the flour, and cook over medium-high heat, whisking, for 1 minute. Whisk in the broth and add the tomatoes and scallions. Bring to a boil, reduce the heat to low, and cook, covered, for 3 minutes. Return the tasso to the sauce, add the lobster meat, and heat through. (Can be made up to 3 hours ahead and set aside, covered, at cool room temperature. Reheat

gently.) Before serving, stir in the parsley and lemon juice. Season with salt and pepper to taste.

3. To make the grits, bring the water to a boil in a large saucepan. Add the salt and slowly stir in the grits. Reduce the heat to low, cover, and cook, stirring occasionally, until thickened, 5 to 7 minutes. Remove from the heat and add the cheese in handfuls, stirring until melted. Stir in the butter and pepper.

4. Spoon the grits onto plates, spoon the lobster mixture over, and serve.

NOTES:

1. Tasso, which is spicy smoked Cajun pork, is great in this dish. If you can't get it, have the deli cut ½-inch slices of smoked ham or use a ham steak or leftover ham.

2. Seafood broth or stock can often be found in supermarkets near the chicken and beef broth. Bottled clam juice is shelved with the canned seafood. If the clam juice is salty, dilute with water. A recipe for Quick Lobster Broth is found on page 15.

3. Cook three 1¼-pound hard-shell lobsters or four 1-pound soft-shells and remove the meat (see chart, page 15) or buy picked-out meat.

Cheese Grits

4 cups water

1 teaspoon salt

1 cup quick-cooking grits

8 ounces sharp cheddar cheese, shredded (2 cups)

3 tablespoons butter

½ teaspoon freshly ground black pepper

4 SERVINGS

Lobster and Red Bliss Hash

1¼ pounds red
skinned potatoes

6 strips bacon

2¼ cups chopped cooked
lobster meat (12 ounces)
(see Note)

⅔ cup thinly
sliced scallions, white
and green parts

½ cup diced red bell pepper

¼ cup chopped
fresh flat-leaf parsley

1 tablespoon fresh thyme
leaves

¾ teaspoon salt

¼ teaspoon freshly ground
black pepper

½ cup cream,
plus more if necessary

3 tablespoons vegetable oil

2 tablespoons butter

Lemon wedges for garnish

~~~~~~~~~~~~~~~~~~~

4 SERVINGS

I adore hash for supper, and what could possibly be better than "hashed" lobster? Serve with a bowl of Dill-Pickled Beet Salad (page 112) and buttered rye toast.

1. Cut the potatoes into rough 2-inch chunks and put them in a large saucepan with cold salted water to cover. Bring to a boil and cook until just tender, 10 to 15 minutes. Drain, and when the potatoes are cool enough to handle, cut into ½-inch dice. You should have about 4 cups.

2. Cook the bacon in a very large (12- to 13-inch) skillet over medium-low heat until crisp and the fat is rendered, 10 to 15 minutes. Remove the bacon with a slotted spoon and drain on paper towels. Pour off the fat but do not wash the pan.

3. Chop the bacon and toss in a large bowl with the potatoes, lobster, scallions, bell pepper, parsley, thyme, salt, and pepper. Drizzle with the cream, adding a tablespoon or two more if the mixture seems dry. (This will depend on the starchiness of the potatoes.) Refrigerate for at least 30 minutes.

4. Add the oil and butter to the unwashed skillet and cook the hash over medium heat until a nice brown crust forms on the bottom, 5 to 8 minutes. Turn in sections with a spatula, press the hash down in the

skillet, and continue to cook until browned on the second side, about 5 minutes longer. Serve the hash garnished with lemon wedges.

NOTE: *Cook two 1½-pound hard-shell lobsters or three 1-pound soft-shells and remove the meat (see chart, page 15) or buy picked-out meat.*

THE MAINE LOBSTER FESTIVAL

The five-day annual event is held in Rockland, Maine, and sports the usual carnival rides, tie-dye shirts, cotton candy, and fried dough — but otherwise this is a festival like no other. Attendees consume 25,000 pounds of lobster dipped in 2,000 pounds of melted butter. While not eating the crustacean, they compete in lobster-cooking contests, take lobster boat rides, participate in a lobster crate race (running over partially submerged lobster crates before plummeting into the ocean), and enjoy a marine-themed parade and the coronation of the Maine Sea Goddess.

Lobster and Sauce

5 tablespoons
extra-virgin olive oil

5 tablespoons butter

4 large garlic cloves, minced

3/4 cup dry white wine

2 (28-ounce) cans plum
tomatoes with juice (see Note)

1 (28-ounce) can
tomato purée

2 tablespoons tomato paste

2 teaspoons sugar

1½ teaspoons red pepper
flakes (see Note)

1 teaspoon salt

½ teaspoon freshly
ground black pepper

¼ cup chopped
fresh oregano

4 small (1–1¼ pounds)
live lobsters, rinsed

¼ cup chopped
fresh flat-leaf parsley

~~~~~~~~~~~~~~~~~~~~~

Ingredients continue opposite

Lobster Fra Diavolo

There are a number of different fra diavolo techniques, some of which are quite involved, but all are aimed at infusing the spicy (*diavolo* means "devil") sauce with as much lobster flavor as possible. This recipe is simplicity itself, the only daunting part for some people being dispatching the lobsters just before they go into the sauce. You can serve this over pasta, but I think it's easier (and tastier) to let the fabulous creation stand on its own, accompanied with toasted country bread to sop up the sauce. Provide bibs if you can, and pass finger bowls at the end of the meal.

1. Heat the oil and butter in a very large pot. Add the garlic and cook over medium heat, stirring, for 1 minute. Add the wine, bring to a boil, and cook briskly until reduced by about half, 3 to 4 minutes. Add the tomatoes, purée, and tomato paste, and use kitchen scissors, a potato masher, or the side of a spoon to break the whole tomatoes into small pieces. Add the sugar, pepper flakes, salt, and black pepper, and bring to a boil again. Reduce the heat to low and simmer, uncovered, until the sauce is quite thick, about 1 hour. Stir in the oregano. (Can be made up to 2 days ahead and refrigerated.)

2. Follow the directions for splitting live lobsters on page 16. Remove the intestinal veins and head sacs but leave some of the tomalley in the bodies

for flavor. If the lobsters are females, leave the shiny black roe in the bodies.

3. Bring the sauce to a simmer. Add the halved lobsters to the sauce and bring to a boil. Reduce the heat to low and cook, covered, for 20 minutes. Turn off the heat and let the pot stand for 30 minutes to 1 hour to infuse the sauce with lobster flavor.

4. To make the toasts, preheat the oven to 375 degrees. Brush the bread slices with olive oil, season with salt and pepper to taste, and lay them out on a baking sheet. Bake for about 10 minutes, until the toasts are golden brown.

5. When ready to serve, gently reheat the lobster. Spoon the sauce into shallow bowls, add two lobster halves to each bowl, and sprinkle with parsley. Pass bread for mopping up the sauce. Provide plenty of paper napkins and nutcrackers and lobster picks for extracting the meat. Provide finger bowls (see Note) and cloth napkins after the meal.

NOTES:

1. Use top-quality Italian plum tomatoes such as San Marzano, which are now readily available in supermarkets.

2. This amount of pepper flakes will make a moderately spicy sauce. Adjust amounts to your own taste.

3. For finger bowls, fill attractive bowls with warm water, float a lemon slice on top, and offer each guest a cloth napkin.

Toasted Country Bread

Sliced Italian or other crusty bread

Extra-virgin olive oil

Salt and freshly ground pepper

4 SERVINGS

LOBSTER BOAT LOVE

"Mortgaged or not, The Wooden Nickel looks good out there, just the shape he goes for, boat or woman: high-stemmed, low freeboard amidships, good broad stern so she'll ride easy in a following sea."

William Carpenter, *The Wooden Nickel*

Ritzy Lobster Pie

1 cup (2 sticks) butter

2 cups crushed Ritz crackers

2 teaspoons lobster tomalley, if available (optional) (see Note)

2 teaspoons grated lemon zest

2 tablespoons lemon juice

1/2 cup seafood broth or clam juice (see Note)

Salt and freshly ground black pepper

3 cups coarsely chopped cooked lobster meat (1 pound) (see Note)

Fresh parsley sprigs for garnish

Lemon wedges for garnish

~~~~~~~~~~~~~~~~~

4 SERVINGS

Crushed Ritz crackers make a simply wonderful topping or stuffing for almost any seafood, including this classic lobster pie, which is an adaptation of the dish served at the Maine Diner in Wells. A bowl of Dill-Pickled Beet Salad (page 112) is great on the side, and slim wedges of Chocolate Silk Pie (page 132) would be the right dessert.

1. Melt ¾ cup (1½ sticks) of the butter in a large skillet. Add the cracker crumbs and cook over medium-high heat, stirring often, until very lightly toasted, about 2 minutes. Stir in the tomalley, if desired. Add the lemon zest and juice and stir in the broth, tossing to combine. Season with salt and pepper to taste.

2. Divide the lobster meat among four 12- to 16-ounce ramekins or strew in the bottom of a shallow 1½-quart baking dish. Cover with the cracker mixture, patting it on evenly. (The casseroles can be prepared up to 8 hours ahead and refrigerated. Remove from the refrigerator 1 hour or so before baking.)

3. Preheat the oven to 425 degrees.

4. Bake the casserole(s) until the top begins to brown and the lobster is heated through, 10 to 15 minutes. Garnish with parsley and lemon wedges and serve the remaining 4 tablespoons butter, melted, alongside for spooning onto the lobster meat.

NOTES:

1. *The green lobster tomalley (sometimes likened to the lobster liver) adds a real boost of lobster flavor, but the pies are also delicious without it.*

2. *Seafood broth or stock can often be found in super-markets near the chicken and beef broth. Bottled clam juice is shelved with the canned seafood. If the clam juice is salty, dilute with water.*

3. *Cook three 1¼-pound hard-shell lobsters or four 1-pound soft-shells and remove the meat (see chart, page 15) or buy picked-out meat.*

LAZY MAN'S LOBSTER

It's a very popular menu item (and why not, when all the work is done for you?), but if made at home, the cook has got to love the eater a lot. Pick out the meat from one or more cooked lobsters, and strew in the bottom of a gratin or other baking dish. Drizzle with melted butter, sprinkle with paprika, and bake in a preheated 350-degree oven until warmed. Serve with lemon wedges.

Lobster Pot Pies
with Puff Pastry Hats

Ramekins hold nuggets of lobster nestled in a sherry-and-tarragon-laced cream sauce and are topped with a crisp puff pastry "hat." Complete this elegant meal with a mesclun salad strewn with toasted pecans and gorgonzola and perhaps Chocolate Bread and Butter Pudding with Rum Custard Sauce (page 134) for dessert.

1. Melt the butter in a large skillet or saucepan. Add the leeks and carrots and cook, covered, over medium-low heat, stirring occasionally, until the carrots are tender, 10 to 15 minutes. Sprinkle on the flour, raise the heat to high, and cook, stirring, for 1 minute. Add the broth and cream, bring to a boil, and cook, stirring, until the sauce is smooth and thickened, about 3 minutes. Stir in the sherry, lemon zest, and tarragon, and season with the salt, black pepper, and cayenne.

2. Distribute the lobster in the bottoms of four buttered 12- to 16-ounce ramekins, scatter with the peas, and pour the sauce over. Cover and refrigerate for at least 1 hour or up to 8 hours.

3. On a lightly floured board, roll out the puff pastry to a 9- by 13-inch rectangle. Cut out shapes slightly smaller than the interior of the ramekins, arrange on a baking sheet, and place in the freezer until ready to bake.

Recipe continues on next page

5 tablespoons butter

2 cups thinly sliced leeks, white and light green parts only

3/4 cup finely diced carrots

3 tablespoons all-purpose flour

1 1/2 cups seafood broth or clam juice (see Note)

1/2 cup heavy cream

3 tablespoons dry sherry

1 tablespoon grated lemon zest

1 tablespoon chopped fresh tarragon

1 teaspoon salt

1/4 teaspoon freshly ground black pepper

1/8 teaspoon cayenne pepper

3 cups roughly chopped cooked lobster meat (1 pound) (see Note)

3/4 cup tiny frozen peas

1 sheet frozen puff pastry, thawed but well chilled

1 egg, lightly beaten with 1 tablespoon water

4 SERVINGS

④ Preheat the oven to 425 degrees.

⑤ Uncover the ramekins, place the cut-out puff pastry atop the sauce, and brush the pastry with the egg wash. Bake for 10 minutes, then reduce the oven temperature to 375 degrees and bake for 25 to 30 minutes more, until the pastry is deep golden brown and puffed and the filling is hot and bubbly. Let the pot pies cool slightly and serve.

NOTES:

1. Seafood broth or stock can often be found in supermarkets near the chicken and beef broth. Bottled clam juice is shelved with the canned seafood. If the clam juice is salty, dilute with water. A recipe for Quick Lobster Broth is found on page 15.

2. Cook three 1¼-pound hard-shell lobsters or four 1-pound soft-shells and remove the meat (see chart, page 15) or buy picked-out meat.

EAT IT ALL

"Any meat you can pull, squeeze, or suck from a lobster will taste good."

Jasper White,
Cooking from
New England

CHAPTER FIVE

ROLLS, TACOS, PIZZAS, AND SANDWICHES

Deluxe Lobster Club on Brioche with Saffron Mayo

Anne Rosenzweig came up with a brilliant conceit when she created the magnificent lobster club sandwich on buttery brioche for her New York restaurant Arcadia in the 1980s. I have taken it one step further with the addition of the saffron mayo — which, if you're not partial to this pungent seasoning, you can skip, of course.

1. Combine the vinegar and saffron in a small saucepan. Heat gently for 1 to 2 minutes, using the back of a spoon to help crush and dissolve the saffron. Whisk the saffron vinegar into the 3 tablespoons of mayonnaise. Toss the lobster meat with the saffron mayo, season with salt and pepper to taste, and refrigerate. (Can be made up to 4 hours ahead.)

2. Cook the bacon in a skillet over medium-low heat until the fat is rendered and the bacon is crisp, 10 to 15 minutes (or cook it in a microwave). Remove the bacon with a slotted spoon and drain on paper towels.

3. Spread plain mayonnaise on each of the toasted bread slices. Layer on lettuce leaves, then the lobster salad, and sandwich with a second slice of bread, mayonnaise side up. Layer tomato and bacon on top of the second bread slice, and then top with a third slice of bread.

Recipe continues on next page

2 teaspoons white wine vinegar

¼ teaspoon saffron threads, crumbled

3 tablespoons mayonnaise, plus more for spreading

1 cup chopped cooked lobster meat (5 ounces) (see Note)

Salt and freshly ground black pepper

6 strips bacon

6 or more thin slices brioche or challah (see Note), lightly toasted

Several leaves crisp lettuce, such as romaine

1 medium-large ripe tomato, sliced

〜〜〜〜〜〜〜〜〜

2 SERVINGS

4 Cut the sandwiches in half diagonally, skewer with a toothpick to hold the layers together, and serve.

NOTES:

1. Cook one 1¼-pound hard-shell lobster or two 1-pound soft-shells and remove the meat (see chart, page 15) or buy picked-out meat.

2. The number of bread slices depends on the size of the loaf. Challah is often shaped into a long braid, so you could make twice as many small sandwiches or try slicing on the diagonal to make larger slices.

WHY TOP-LOAD?

A conventional hot dog roll has a crust on top and is split through the side. The New England top-split roll (also called "soft-sided" or "top-loaded") is cut right down through the top crust so that both sides of the roll are crustless. No one really knows why top-split roll are traditional in New England, but my personal theory is that not only is this a great bun for hot dogs, but it makes a superior receptacle for lobster and other seafood fillings. The crustless sides are brushed with butter and griddle-toasted and the filling nestles into the soft center, which absorbs all the wonderful juices and flavors.

CLASSIC LOBSTER ROLLS TWO WAYS

Lobster Salad Roll

This mayonnaise-based salad filling is the most common lobster-roll formula. Note the addition of nothing more than salt, pepper, and a squeeze of lemon juice, allowing for the pure, sea-fresh taste of lobster meat to shine through. New England–style top-split hot dog rolls are ideal for lobster rolls (see sidebar, facing page), but if top-split rolls aren't available, use conventional hot dog rolls, grilling the crusty top and bottom, not the interior. Potato chips and Calico Vinegar Slaw (page 106) are the right sides.

1. Toss the lobster with the lemon juice in a bowl. Add the mayonnaise and stir to combine, adding more if necessary to moisten the salad sufficiently. Season with salt and pepper, going easy on the pepper. Refrigerate until ready to make the rolls.

2. Heat a cast-iron griddle or large skillet over medium heat. Brush the crustless sides of the rolls with melted butter and cook on the griddle, turning once, until both sides are golden brown, about 2 minutes per side.

3. Open the rolls and spoon in the lobster salad, heaping it high. Serve immediately.

NOTE: *Cook two 1¼-pound hard-shell lobsters or three 1-pound soft-shells and remove the meat (see chart, page 15) or buy picked-out meat.*

Classic Lobster Rolls continue on the next page

2 cups cooked lobster meat, cut into chunks no smaller than about ¾ inch (about 10 ounces) (see Note)

2 teaspoons lemon juice

⅓ cup mayonnaise, plus more if necessary

Salt and freshly ground black pepper

4 top-split hot dog rolls

4 tablespoons butter, melted

4 SERVINGS

Hot Lobster Roll

6 tablespoons butter

4 top-split hot dog rolls

2 cups cooked lobster meat, cut or torn into 1- to 2-inch pieces (about 10 ounces) (see Note)

Lemon wedges for garnish

~~~~~~~~~~~~~~~~~

4 SERVINGS

Sometimes called a Connecticut-style roll, this sandwich is nothing more than hefty chunks of butter-drenched lobster meat heaped into a top-split bun. Some say it was the invention of a loyal customer at Perry's restaurant in Milford, Connecticut, sometime in the 1920s, and its popularity spread, making it the lobster roll standard throughout that state and also on Long Island. Creamy Coleslaw (page 104) and potato chips are called for as accompaniments.

1. Melt the butter in a medium-large skillet.

2. Heat a cast-iron griddle or a second skillet over medium heat. Brush the crustless sides of the rolls with some of the melted butter, and cook on the griddle, turning once, until both sides are golden brown, about 2 minutes per side.

3. Toss the lobster meat with the remaining melted butter in the other skillet over medium heat just until warm, about 1 minute.

4. Open the rolls, spoon in the buttered lobster meat, and garnish with a lemon wedge.

NOTE: *Cook two 1¼-pound hard-shell lobsters or three 1-pound soft-shells and remove the meat (see chart, page 15) or buy picked-out meat.*

Lobster Melts

These quick open-face sandwiches are the perfect way to use a bit of leftover lobster. The sandwiches are great with New Potato Salad with Egg and Pickle (page 108).

1. Toss the lobster in a bowl with the mayonnaise, parsley, shallots, and lemon juice. Season with a dash of the hot pepper sauce. Refrigerate the mixture until ready to make the sandwiches.

2. Preheat the broiler and place a rack about 4 inches from the heating element.

3. Lightly toast the bread. Spread the toasts with the lobster salad, top with tomato slices, and sprinkle with cheese. Transfer to a baking sheet and broil until the cheese is bubbly and pale golden brown, 2 to 3 minutes.

NOTE: *Cook one 1¼-pound hard-shell lobster or two 1-pound soft-shells and remove the meat (see chart, page 15) or buy picked-out meat.*

1 cup diced cooked lobster meat (about 5 ounces) (see Note)

1½ tablespoons mayonnaise

1 tablespoon chopped fresh flat-leaf parsley

2 teaspoons minced shallots

1 teaspoon lemon juice

Liquid hot pepper sauce

2–4 slices (depending on size) firm sandwich bread

1 small tomato, sliced

2 ounces sharp cheddar cheese, shredded (½ cup)

2 SERVINGS

Lobster and Arugula Pizza

1¼ pounds pizza dough
(see Note)

Semolina or cornmeal
(see Note)

1 pound tomatoes,
cored and thinly sliced

4 ounces prosciutto,
chopped

2 tablespoons extra-virgin
olive oil, plus 1 tablespoon
for arugula

Salt and freshly
ground black pepper

1½ cups chopped
cooked lobster meat
(8 ounces) (see Note)

6 ounces shredded
mozzarella (1½ cups)

2 cups arugula

2 teaspoons
balsamic vinegar

~~~~~~~~~~~~~~~~~~~

MAKES 2 PIZZAS,
2-3 SERVINGS EACH

Not that making pizza dough is difficult, but it does involve some advance planning, so I usually take the easy way out and use store-bought pizza crust — either uncooked dough or good-quality prebaked rounds.

1. Place a pizza stone in the oven and preheat the oven to 450 degrees for at least 30 minutes (see Note). Divide the dough in half and pull and stretch one piece into an 11- to 12-inch oval. Place the dough on a pizza peel or rimless cookie sheet that has been coated with semolina or cornmeal. Arrange half the tomatoes in concentric circles over the dough, scatter with half the prosciutto, drizzle with 1 tablespoon of the oil, and sprinkle with salt and pepper. Slide the dough round onto the pizza stone and bake for about 10 minutes, until the dough just begins to brown.

2. Remove the pizza from the oven and scatter with half the lobster and half the mozzarella. Return to the oven and bake for 5 to 8 minutes longer, until the cheese is melted and speckled with brown.

3. Repeat with the second piece of pizza dough.

4. Toss the arugula with the remaining 1 tablespoon oil and the vinegar. Top the pizzas with the dressed arugula, cut into wedges, and serve.

NOTES:

1. You can substitute a prebaked pizza round. Top with all the ingredients except the arugula and bake for about 10 minutes. Semolina is the best choice because the perfectly round grains create good sliding action for the dough. If you don't have a pizza stone you can still produce a reasonably crisp-bottomed pizza by shaping and stretching the dough on an oiled pizza pan or baking sheet.

2. Cook one 1½-pound hard-shell lobster or two 1-pound soft-shells and remove the meat (see chart, page 15) or buy picked-out meat.

WORLD'S LONGEST LOBSTER ROLL

The longest ever lobster roll, measuring 61 feet, 9½ inches, secured a Guinness World Record in 2010. Designed as a fundraiser for needy children, the mammoth roll ran down a considerable stretch of Commercial Street at Portland, Maine's Old Port Festival.

Lobster Quesadillas
with Chunky Guacamole

Guacamole

1 ripe avocado

¼ cup finely diced red onion

2 teaspoons grated lime zest

2 tablespoons lime juice

¼ cup chopped fresh cilantro

Salt and freshly ground black pepper

~~~~~~~~~~~~~~~~

Quesadillas

1½ cups shredded pepper Jack cheese (see Note)

1 cup cooked lobster meat, chopped medium-fine (about 5 ounces) (see Note)

8 (6-inch) flour tortillas

About 3 tablespoons vegetable oil

~~~~~~~~~~~~~~~~

3 TO 4 SERVINGS, DEPENDING ON APPETITES

This is a wonderful way to repurpose a bit of leftover lobster. Serve the quesadillas for lunch or as a light supper, in which case you might want to offer two per person. Accompany with a salad of shredded lettuce and radishes topped with a creamy ranch-style dressing.

1. To make the guacamole, pit and peel the avocado and cut the flesh into chunks. Combine in a bowl with the onion, lime zest and juice, and cilantro. Use a large fork or a potato masher to coarsely mash the avocado, leaving some chunks visible. Season with salt and pepper to taste. (Can be made up to 2 hours ahead. If held any longer the avocado will darken.)

2. To make the quesadillas, toss the cheese and lobster together in a bowl. Place four tortillas on a work surface and divide the lobster mixture among them, spreading it out evenly. Top each with a second tortilla, pressing together firmly.

3. Heat a large skillet over medium-high heat. Brush both sides of the quesadillas with oil and cook, in batches, until the cheese melts and the tortillas are crisp and golden, 1½ to 2 minutes per side.

4. Cut the quesadillas into wedges and serve, topped with guacamole.

NOTES:

1. If you can't get pepper Jack use plain Monterey Jack cheese and add half of a finely minced jalapeño pepper.

2. Cook one 1¼-pound hard-shell lobster or two 1-pound soft-shells and remove the meat (see chart, page 15) or buy picked-out meat.

QUINTESSENTIAL CLAM SHACKS

The New England and Long Island coastlines are dotted with summer-time outdoor eateries affectionately known as "clam shacks." Clam shacks are usually bare bones walk-away venues, with one window for ordering your food and another where you pick it up. Communal picnic tables are sometimes scattered here and there or sometimes you munch your lobster or clam roll leaning against your car. Freshly fried seafood — especially fried whole-belly clams — reigns supreme, but other options such as lobster and crabmeat salad rolls and burgers, hot dogs, fries, and coleslaw are menu standards.

Lobster Soft Tacos

I like to put out bowls of all the fixings and let people craft their own tacos. Tortillas can be heated in a microwave or one at a time in a hot skillet. To round out the meal, think refried beans or pinto beans spiked with vinegar and topped with cheese.

1. Toss the lobster with the lime juice in a small bowl.

2. Warm the tortillas.

3. For each taco, spread a layer of sliced avocado, mashing it slightly if desired, on a tortilla. Season with salt and pepper and add a drizzle of hot sauce or dollop of salsa. Add a layer of lobster and scatter with cabbage, cheese, and cilantro. Squeeze additional lime juice over the tops if desired, roll up, and eat.

NOTES:

1. Cook two 1¼-pound hard-shell lobsters or three 1-pound soft-shells and remove the meat (see chart, page 15) or buy picked-out meat.

2. Several companies produce shredded Mexican cheese blends, which include such cheese varieties as Monterey Jack, mild cheddar, queso quesadilla, and asadero.

2 cups chopped cooked lobster meat (10 ounces) (see Note)

2 tablespoons lime juice

8–12 (6-inch) corn tortillas

2 ripe avocados, pitted, peeled, and sliced

Salt and freshly ground black pepper

Hot sauce or fresh salsa

1 cup finely shredded cabbage

1½ cups shredded mixed Mexican cheeses (see Note)

¾ cup fresh cilantro sprigs, stemmed

Lime wedges (optional)

3–4 SERVINGS, DEPENDING ON APPETITES

IN-THE-ROUGH PROTOCOL

Lobster pound eateries still dot the Maine coast and some are scattered along inland tourist highways, where the lobsters are now stored in tanks. Some cookers are still wood-fired, though most use propane.

⚓ Dress casually (wear a good blouse at your peril) and bring a sweater and bug spray.

⚓ Step up to the window to place your order. Your lobster is then placed in a sturdy string bag along with corn, steamers, or mussels and the bag goes into the cooker.

⚓ Take a place at a picnic table and wait 20 minutes or so. Sip on wine or a beer (many pounds are BYOB) and people-watch or admire the landscape.

⚓ Dinner will be delivered on sturdy paper plates. For a fancier occasion, bring your own linen, plates, glasses, and flatware.

⚓ Tie on a bib, roll up your sleeves, pick up a lobster cracker, and get to work.

⚓ Satiated, use a wet wipe to clean lobstery hands.

⚓ Order blueberry pie.

⚓ Don't forget to bus your tray.

CHAPTER SIX

SIDES

Calico Vinegar Slaw

½ medium head green cabbage

1 carrot, peeled

½ red bell pepper

1 small sweet red or white onion

⅓ cup sugar

⅓ cup white wine vinegar

½ cup vegetable oil

1 teaspoon salt, plus more if necessary

¼ teaspoon celery seed

Freshly ground black pepper

~~~~~~~~~~~~~~~~

6–8 SERVINGS

Sweet-tart vinegary slaw is the perfect foil for many lobster preparations, including lobster rolls, lobster stew, and a plain steamed lobster shore dinner. The carrot and bell pepper add beautiful color as well as flavor.

1. Use the food processor or a large knife to cut the cabbage into shreds. You should have about 7 cups. Grate the carrot in the food processor or on a box grater. Cut the bell pepper and onion into very thin slices and cut the slices in half crosswise. Toss all the vegetables together in a large bowl.

2. Whisk the sugar and vinegar together in a small bowl until most of the sugar is dissolved. Whisk in the oil, salt, and celery seed. Pour the dressing over the cabbage mixture and toss well. Refrigerate for at least 1 hour or for up to 6 hours.

3. Before serving, drain off any excess liquid, stir the coleslaw, and season with pepper and additional salt if necessary.

New Potato Salad

with Egg and Pickle

2 eggs

2 pounds waxy potatoes
such as Yukon golds
or red-skinned, cut into
2-inch chunks

3 tablespoons
sweet pickle juice

Salt and freshly ground
black pepper

2/3 cup mayonnaise, plus
more if necessary

2 tablespoons Dijon mustard

2 tablespoons whole
milk or cream

3/4 cup finely chopped
celery

1/2 cup finely chopped red or
sweet white onion

2 tablespoons chopped
gherkins or sweet pickles

2 tablespoons minced
fresh flat-leaf parsley or dill
or a combination

~~~~~~~~~~~~~~~~~

6–8 SERVINGS

Everyone needs a tried-and-true potato salad recipe, and this is mine. It has nice celery crunch, just enough onion, and a pleasing hint of sweetness from the pickle juice. I love the flavor and color provided by chopped hard-boiled eggs, but omit them if you prefer. To dress up the salad, present it on a bed of lettuce and garnish with tomato wedges and/or sliced radishes.

1. Place the eggs in a small saucepan and cover with cold water. Bring to a rolling boil, cover, remove from the heat, and let stand for 10 minutes. Drain the eggs and run under cold water to cool. Peel the eggs and coarsely chop.

2. Put the potatoes in a large pot of salted water, bring to a boil, and cook until just fork-tender, about 15 minutes. Drain well. When cool enough to handle, slip off the peels and cut the potato into 1/2-inch cubes. (You should have about 8 cups.)

3. Toss the potatoes in a large bowl with the pickle juice and about 1/2 teaspoon each of salt and pepper. Set aside to cool for about 15 minutes.

4. Whisk the mayonnaise with the mustard and milk in a medium bowl. Stir in the celery, onion, pickles, and the chopped eggs. Pour the dressing over the potatoes, stir gently to combine, and refrigerate for at least 1 hour or for up to 24 hours.

5 Before serving, stir again to redistribute the dressing, adding more mayonnaise if it seems dry, and adjust the seasonings if necessary. Sprinkle with the herbs and serve.

LOBSTER POLITICIAN

Dureyea's Lobster Deck and Seafood in Montauk, Long Island, is currently run by the third generation of Dureyeas. During the mid-twentieth century, the family spawned a politician, Perry Dureyea Jr., who was a 20-year member of the New York State Assembly and ran for governor before returning to his family's wholesale lobster and fish business.

Tomato, Watermelon, and Feta Salad

2 pounds yellow or red tomatoes, seeded and cut into rough 3/4- to 1-inch dice (about 4 cups)

3 pounds seedless watermelon, removed from rind and cut into rough 3/4- to 1-inch dice (about 4 cups)

1 3/4 cups peeled, seeded, and chopped cucumber (from one small cucumber)

6 ounces feta cheese, diced or coarsely crumbled (about 1 1/2 cups)

1/4 cup shredded fresh mint leaves, plus sprigs for garnish

4-5 tablespoons Simple Vinaigrette (page 105)

Salt and freshly ground black pepper

4-6 SERVINGS

Feta contributes its salty bite to this lovely toss of tomato and watermelon. This salad is especially delicious after a steamed lobster dinner.

Gently toss the tomatoes, watermelon, cucumber, feta, and mint together in a large bowl. Drizzle with the dressing, toss again, and season with salt and pepper to taste. Garnish with mint sprigs and serve immediately.

OCEAN COWBOYS

"The Double Trouble *[lobster boat] skidded, bounced, and bucked her way south into the open ocean. It is sometimes said that lobstermen are the cowboys of the American East. The resemblance can be striking."*

Trevor Corson, *The Secret Life of Lobsters*

Composed Salad of Tomatoes, Blueberries, and Goat Cheese

Blueberries are perfectly paired with tomatoes, creamy goat cheese, and chopped almonds. This makes a lovely first course before a lobster main course.

1. Spread the arugula on a platter. Spread the sliced tomatoes over the arugula and scatter with the blueberries. Dab clumps of goat cheese evenly over the blueberries and scatter with the almonds. (Can be prepared up to 3 hours ahead and refrigerated.)

2. Drizzle with vinaigrette and season with additional salt and pepper to taste.

NOTE: *Whole almonds seasoned with tamari can usually be found in the whole foods section of the supermarket. Roasted salted almonds are shelved with the snack foods.*

4 handfuls of arugula leaves

4 medium ripe tomatoes, cored and sliced (about 2 pounds)

2 cups blueberries

4 ounces soft goat cheese

2/3 cup chopped tamari almonds or roasted salted almonds (see Note)

4–5 tablespoons Simple Vinaigrette (page 105)

Salt and freshly ground black pepper

4 SERVINGS

Dill-Pickled Beet Salad

1½ pounds beets of uniform size, trimmed

¾ cup cider vinegar

⅓ cup sugar

¼ cup water

½ teaspoon salt

½ teaspoon dill seeds

3 tablespoons Simple Vinaigrette (page 105)

1 tablespoon chopped fresh dill

4 SERVINGS

Pickled beets are a simple, old-fashioned mainstay; they are always a welcome addition to any meal, summer or winter. Here, they are dressed up with a drizzle of vinaigrette and shower of chopped fresh dill.

1. Bring a large pot of salted water to a boil and cook the beats until they are tender when pierced with a sharp knife, 30 to 45 minutes, depending on size. Drain, and when cool enough to handle, peel and slice into a bowl.

2. Combine the vinegar, sugar, water, salt, and dill seeds in a small saucepan and bring to a boil. Cook, stirring, until the sugar dissolves, about 1 minute. Pour the hot liquid over the beets and stir gently to coat the beets. Cool to room temperature, and then cover and refrigerate for at least 1 hour or for up to a week.

3. To serve, spoon the beets out of the pickling liquid and place in a shallow bowl. Drizzle with the vinaigrette and sprinkle with fresh dill.

CHAPTER SEVEN

A LEMON, BERRY, OR CHOCOLATE FINISH

Best Blueberry Pie

Flaky Pie Pastry

2½ cups all-purpose flour

1 teaspoon salt

1 teaspoon sugar

½ cup (1 stick) cold unsalted butter, cut into 8 pieces

½ cup cold vegetable shortening, cut into 8 chunks

6–8 tablespoons ice water

~~~~~~~~~

MAKES PASTRY FOR
1 DOUBLE-CRUST PIE

~~~~~~~~~

Filling

4½ cups blueberries

¾ cup sugar

2½ tablespoons
all-purpose flour

1 tablespoon lemon juice

¼ teaspoon
ground cinnamon

⅛ teaspoon salt

Ingredients continue opposite

This classic blueberry pie is delicious made with large high-bush berries, but if you have access to the tiny, tart low-bush blueberries from Maine, they make a superior filling. Additional flavorings are only a smidgen of cinnamon and a little lemon juice to bring out the flavor of the berries. Because the deep purpley blue of the berry filling is so gorgeous, this pie is especially lovely with a woven lattice crust (see Note).

1. To make the pastry, combine the flour, salt, and sugar in a food processor. Pulse to mix. Distribute the butter and shortening over the flour and process in short bursts until most of the shortening is about the size of small peas. Sprinkle 6 tablespoons of the ice water over the mixture and pulse just until no dry flour remains and the dough begins to clump together. If the dough is too dry, sprinkle on the remaining 2 tablespoons water and pulse again.

2. Divide the dough in half and turn out onto two sheets of plastic wrap. Shape and flatten into two 5-inch discs, wrap, and refrigerate for at least 30 minutes. Remove from the refrigerator 10 minutes before rolling out.

3. To assemble the pie, preheat the oven to 425 degrees.

4. On a floured surface, roll out half the dough to a 12-inch round. Ease into a 9-inch pie plate.

5 Toss the blueberries in a large bowl with the sugar, flour, lemon juice, cinnamon, and salt. Scrape into the prepared pie shell and distribute the butter over the fruit.

6 Roll out the second dough disc to a 12-inch round and place over the fruit (see Note). Trim the overhanging dough to ¾ inch all around. Turn the edges under and flute or crimp the dough to seal. Use a sharp knife to slash several steam vents in the crust.

7 Bake for 30 minutes. Reduce the oven temperature to 350 degrees and bake for an additional 25 to 35 minutes, until the crust is golden and berry juices bubble through the vents. Cool on a wire rack. Serve slightly warm or at room temperature, accompanied by a scoop of vanilla ice cream, if desired.

NOTE: *For a lattice, cut the rolled-out top crust into ½-inch-wide strips and, starting in the center, interweave the strips into a lattice. (Consult a good reference, such as* The Joy of Cooking, *1997, for illustrations.) Turn the edges under and flute as above.*

1 tablespoon unsalted butter, cut into several pieces

Vanilla ice cream (optional)

MAKES ONE 9-INCH PIE, 8–10 SERVINGS

THE LOBSTER INSTITUTE

Working with lobster-men and other sectors of the lobster industry from Long Island Sound to Newfoundland, the mission of the Lobster Institute is to sustain a viable lobster fishery through conservation, research, and education. It is the only international organization of its kind.

Rustic Summer Fruit Tart

You can make this versatile hand-shaped tart with just about any summer berry (or a combination thereof) or with sliced peaches or other stone fruits. A layer of sliced almonds hides beneath the fruit, contributing additional richness. The tart requires no special pan or equipment and emerges from the oven with a pleasingly homespun, rustic look.

1. To make the pastry, combine the flour, granulated sugar, and salt in a food processor. Pulse to mix. Distribute the butter over the flour and process in short bursts until the bits of butter are about the size of small peas. Sprinkle 3 tablespoons of the ice water over the mixture and pulse just until no dry flour remains and the dough begins to clump together. If the dough is too dry, sprinkle on the remaining 1 tablespoon water and pulse again.

2. Turn out onto a sheet of plastic wrap, gather into a ball, flatten into a 5-inch disc, and refrigerate for at least 30 minutes.

3. To make the filling, toss the blueberries or other fruit with the granulated sugar, cornstarch, lemon juice, and cinnamon in a large bowl.

4. Preheat the oven to 425 degrees. On a lightly floured surface, roll the pastry out to a 13-inch round. Do not trim the edges; leaving them ragged gives the tart its rustic look. Transfer the pastry to a large rimmed

Recipe continues on next page

Sweet Butter Pastry

1¼ cups all-purpose flour

2 teaspoons granulated sugar

½ teaspoon salt

½ cup (1 stick) cold unsalted butter, cut into small pieces

3–4 tablespoons ice water

~~~~~~~~~~~~

Filling

2½ cups blueberries or fruit combination (see Note)

½ cup granulated sugar

2 tablespoons cornstarch

1 teaspoon lemon juice

¼ teaspoon ground cinnamon

1 egg beaten with 2 teaspoons water

⅓ cup sliced almonds, plus a few for topping

Ingredients continue on next page

1 tablespoon cold unsalted
butter, cut into small pieces

Confectioners' sugar

Vanilla ice cream (optional)

~~~~~~~~~~~~~

MAKES ONE 9-INCH TART,
6–8 SERVINGS

~~~~~~~~~~~~~~~~~~~

JASPER WHITE'S SUMMER SHACKS

Jasper White's Summer Shack restaurants — big, informal, funky, family-friendly, and fun — go through at least 250,000 pounds of lobster every year. Jasper has four Summer Shacks in Massachusetts and one at Mohegan Sun casino in Connecticut.

~~~~~~~~~~~~~~~~~

baking sheet, patching any tears by pressing the dough together with your fingers. Brush the pastry with the egg glaze and sprinkle with the ⅓ cup almonds. Spoon the fruit filling onto the dough, mounding it slightly higher in the center and leaving a 2-inch border all around the edge. Fold the border in, pleating it as necessary to make an uneven 1½-inch-wide folded edge. Scatter the butter over the fruit, brush the edges of the crust with the egg glaze, and sprinkle a few almonds on the edges.

5 Bake for 15 minutes. Reduce the oven temperature to 375 degrees and continue to bake for 25 to 30 minutes, until the pastry is golden brown, the fruit is soft, and the juices are bubbly. Use a large spatula to transfer to a wire rack to cool.

6 Sprinkle with confectioners' sugar and serve slightly warm or at room temperature, with scoops of ice cream if desired.

NOTE: *You can make this tart with just blueberries or other fruit combinations such as blueberries and raspberries, or blueberries and sliced peaches.*

LOBSTER WARS

"According to the laws of Maine, any man with a lobstering license may put a trap anywhere in Maine waters. That's what the laws say. The reality is different. Certain families fish certain territories because they have always done so; certain areas belong to certain islands because they always have; certain waterways are under the control of certain people because they always have been. The ocean, though not marked by fences and deeds, is strictly marked by traditions.... The barriers, though invisible, are real, and they are constantly being tested."

Elizabeth Gilbert, *Stern Men*

Fruit Layer

2/3 cup whole-berry cranberry sauce

6 tablespoons unsalted butter, cut into several pieces

6 thin unpeeled orange slices, seeds removed

~~~~~~~~~~~~~

Cake Layer

1/4 cup roughly chopped pecans

3/4 cup all-purpose flour

1 tablespoon cornmeal

3/4 teaspoon baking powder

1/4 teaspoon baking soda

1/4 teaspoon salt

3 eggs

3/4 cup granulated sugar

1 tablespoon grated orange zest

1/4 cup orange juice

2 teaspoons vanilla extract

Ingredients continue opposite

Cranberry-Orange Upside-Down Cake

Cape Codders finish many a lobster dinner with a cranberry dessert. This cake uses whole-berry cranberry sauce and orange slices for the gorgeous, glistening topping, and the cake layer is an eggy sponge enriched with ground pecans and a tiny bit of cornmeal for a pleasing crumbly texture. The whole gets tied together with orange liqueur–spiked whipped cream.

1. To make the fruit layer, combine the cranberry sauce, butter, and orange slices in a medium saucepan. Bring to a simmer over medium heat, stirring gently, until the cranberry sauce and butter melt. Pour into a 9-inch round cake pan and arrange the oranges to create an even layer.

2. Preheat the oven to 350 degrees.

3. To make the cake, process the pecans in a food processor with about 1 tablespoon of the flour until finely ground. Whisk the nuts with the remaining flour, cornmeal, baking powder, baking soda, and salt in a medium bowl.

4. Using an electric mixer, beat the eggs with the granulated sugar in a large bowl until light and doubled in volume. Beat in the orange zest and juice and vanilla. With the mixer on low speed, add the flour mixture and beat just until combined. Pour the batter over the fruit layer, smoothing the top.

5. Bake for 30 to 35 minutes, until the cake is golden and a tester inserted in the center comes out clean. Cool in the pan for 5 minutes. Run a paring knife around the edge of the cake to loosen it and then immediately invert onto a serving platter. Leave the pan on the cake for a few minutes, and then lift it off. If any topping clings to the pan, simply transfer it to the top of the cake.

6. Whip the cream with the confectioners' sugar and liqueur to soft peaks. Serve the cake warm or at room temperature, topped with the orange cream.

Orange Cream

1 cup chilled heavy cream

¼ cup confectioners' sugar

2 tablespoons orange liqueur

6–8 SERVINGS

MASSACHUSETTS' OWN BERRY

Bay Staters view the cranberry as their very own berry, and with good reason, since Massachusetts has about 900 commercial cranberry operations, more than half of which are located on Cape Cod. It's little wonder that cooks from the Commonwealth like to add cranberries to the menu whenever possible. Cranberries pair brilliantly with lobster, and the two make quite a stunning combination.

Strawberry Shortcake
with Rich Egg Biscuit

Strawberry Filling

2 quarts ripe strawberries

1/3 cup granulated sugar

2 teaspoons lemon juice

~~~~~~~~~~~~~~~~~~~~~~

Egg Biscuit and Topping

2 cups all-purpose flour

1/4 cup granulated sugar

4 teaspoons baking powder

1/2 teaspoon salt

1/2 cup (1 stick) cold unsalted butter, cut into about 12 pieces

1 egg

1/2 cup whole milk

1 1/2 cups chilled heavy cream

2 tablespoons confectioners' sugar

3 tablespoons unsalted butter, softened

~~~~~~~~~~~~~~~~~~~~~~

8 SERVINGS

Strawberry shortcake, made with dead-ripe, fragrant native berries, is probably the queen of all shortcakes. This "short" (meaning very buttery) egg biscuit is baked in one large cake for an impressive presentation. Although shortcake is best served warm, I give instructions for preparing all the elements before guests arrive.

1. Choose eight pretty berries and set them aside for garnish; hull the rest. Place half the hulled berries in a large shallow bowl and crush them with a large fork or a potato masher. Slice the remaining berries and combine with the crushed berries. Stir in the granulated sugar and lemon juice and set aside at room temperature for at least 30 minutes to allow the juices to flow. (Strawberries can be prepared up to 6 hours ahead and refrigerated. Return to room temperature before serving.)

2. To make the biscuit, pulse the flour, granulated sugar, baking powder, and salt in a food processor to blend. Distribute the butter over the flour mixture and pulse until the mixture looks crumbly. Whisk the egg into the milk. With the food-processor motor running, pour the milk mixture through the feed tube and process just until the dough begins to clump together. (To make by hand, whisk the dry ingredients together in a bowl, work in the cold butter with your fingertips, add the milk and egg, and stir with a large

fork to make a soft dough.) Scrape out onto a lightly floured surface, knead lightly a few times, and roll to an 8-inch round. Transfer to a generously buttered 8-inch cake pan. (The dough can be prepared to this point and refrigerated for up to 3 hours.)

3 Preheat the oven to 450 degrees. Place the shortcake in the oven and immediately reduce the oven temperature to 375 degrees. Bake for 22 to 26 minutes, until the cake is pale golden brown on top. Cool in the pan on a rack for 10 minutes.

4 Whip the cream with the confectioners' sugar to soft peaks. (Can be done a couple of hours ahead and refrigerated.)

5 To assemble, transfer the shortcake to a large serving platter. Using a long serrated knife, split the cake horizontally and lift off the top with a large spatula. Spread the bottom layer with the softened butter, spoon on about half the berry mixture, and spread with about half the whipped cream. Replace the top, spoon over the remaining berry mixture, and top with cream. Decorate with the reserved berries. Cut into wedges to serve.

NOTE: *To make individual biscuits, roll the dough to about ¾-inch thickness and cut out 8 biscuits using a 2½-inch cutter. Arrange on a baking sheet and bake for 15 to 18 minutes.*

NORTH SHORE SEAFOOD

David's Fish Market in Salisbury, Massachusetts, is a third-generation operation.

"We try to get everything local — local meaning our territory, which runs about Gloucester to Portland. Our lobster fleet can supply most of what we need except in our busiest months, when we get 'em from Maine."

James Morton

Lemon Blueberry Mousse

3 eggs

1 cup sugar

1 tablespoon lemon zest

½ cup lemon juice

Salt

½ cup (1 stick) unsalted butter, cut into small pieces

1 cup chilled heavy cream

1½ cups blueberries

Fresh mint sprigs for garnish

~~~~~~~~~~~~~~~~~

6 SERVINGS

This is a delicate mousse, light yet rich, which combines lemon *and* berries. I cannot think of a single lobster meal that this wouldn't complement perfectly. The base is a cooked lemon curd, which is yummy on its own, but ethereal when folded with softly whipped cream and berries. If blueberries aren't available, almost any other berry can be substituted.

1. Combine the eggs, sugar, lemon zest and juice, and a pinch of salt in a nonreactive saucepan and whisk, off heat, until light. Place over medium heat, add the butter, and cook, whisking constantly, until the butter melts and the curd thickens and heavily coats the back of a spoon, about 5 minutes. If the curd is lumpy, force it through a strainer. Cover and refrigerate for at least 1 hour, until cold. (Can be made 2 days ahead.)

2. Whip the cream to soft peaks. Whisk about one-third of the whipped cream into the curd to lighten it, and then gently fold the rest of the whipped cream into the lemon mixture. Fold in 1 cup of the blueberries.

3. Spoon the mousse into an attractive glass serving bowl or into individual stemmed glasses. Refrigerate for at least 1 hour or for up to 4 hours. Sprinkle with the remaining ½ cup blueberries and garnish with mint sprigs.

NOTE: *You can substitute purchased lemon curd and add 1 tablespoon grated lemon zest and 2 tablespoons juice. Be sure to buy a good brand such as the curd made by Maine-based Stonewall Kitchen.*

JASPER WHITE ON BLUEBERRY PIE

Noted New England restaurateur and cookbook author Jasper White says, "Blueberry pie holds a place of honor in the food culture of New England. It is expected at certain events: to hold a clambake or lobster dinner and not serve blueberry pie is abnormal. It is more than a dessert — it is an icon. Serve blueberry pie and the world is right; serve it warm with melting vanilla ice cream, and it is nirvana."

Pastry

1¼ cups all-purpose flour

½ teaspoon salt

½ cup (1 stick) cold unsalted butter, cut into small pieces

3–4 tablespoons ice water

~~~~~~~~~~~~~~~~

Filling

2 egg whites

½ teaspoon salt

3 tablespoons plus ⅔ cup sugar

3 tablespoons unsalted butter, softened

2 egg yolks

1 tablespoon all-purpose flour

1 teaspoon grated lemon zest

¾ cup buttermilk

~~~~~~~~~~~~~~~~

8 SERVINGS

Lemon-Buttermilk Sponge Tart

A tart baked in a special French fluted pan always makes such an elegant presentation. This lemony filling is made with buttermilk, which contributes its own additional pleasing tang. It is wonderful on its own or with a sprinkle of berries and is an ideal finish to a lobster dinner.

1. In a food processor, combine the flour and salt. Pulse to mix. Distribute the butter over the flour and process in short bursts until the mixture is about the size of small peas. Sprinkle 3 tablespoons of the ice water over the mixture and pulse just until no dry flour remains and the dough begins to clump together. If the dough is too dry, sprinkle on the remaining 1 tablespoon water and pulse again.

2. Roll the dough out on a lightly floured surface to an 11-inch round. Transfer to a 9½-inch tart pan and fit into the pan, trimming off the top edge. Prick in several places with a fork and place in the freezer for at least 30 minutes.

3. Preheat the oven to 425 degrees.

4. Bake the tart shell directly from the freezer for 14 to 18 minutes, until pale golden. If the pastry puffs up, press the bottom gently with a large flat spatula or an oven-mitted hand to flatten. Fill immediately or cool on a rack. Reduce the oven temperature to 350 degrees.

128

5. To make the filling, beat the egg whites and salt with an electric mixer until frothy. Sprinkle with the 3 tablespoons sugar and beat to soft peaks. Do not wash the beaters. In another bowl, beat the remaining ⅔ cup sugar with the butter until granular and well blended. Beat in the egg yolks, flour, and lemon zest. On low speed, beat in the buttermilk. Stir one-third of the egg whites into the yolk mixture to lighten, and then fold in the remaining whites. Pour the filling into the prepared shell.

6. Bake for 25 to 35 minutes, until the top is golden brown and the custard is set near the center. Cool on a wire rack for at least 1 hour. Serve barely warm or at room temperature, or refrigerate and serve cold.

SLEUTH AT A LOBSTER BAKE

"Pix knew she was a mess. She'd dripped melted butter down her chin as she'd consumed her lobster and clams. Her fingers were sticky from the chicken and corn. Above all she was full — and there was still dessert: blueberry pie and strawberry shortcake, the real kind on a biscuit."

Katherine Hall Page, *The Body in the Basement*

Mocha-Chocolate Chip Shortbread Cookies

1 tablespoon instant coffee or espresso powder

1 tablespoon boiling water

1 cup (2 sticks) unsalted butter, slightly softened

2/3 cup confectioners' sugar

1/4 teaspoon salt

1/2 teaspoon vanilla extract

2 cups all-purpose flour

3/4 cup finely chopped semisweet chocolate or mini semisweet chocolate morsels

~~~~~~~~~~~~~

MAKES ABOUT
4 DOZEN COOKIES

These scrumptious cookies are adapted from Dorie Greenspan's wonderful book *Baking: From My Home to Yours*. Dorie's recipes are always spot-on, and her tips, such as this instruction to roll the soft dough inside a sealed plastic bag, are invaluable. The cookies are rich but not too sweet and are great with a platter of summer fruits.

1. Dissolve the coffee powder in the boiling water and set aside to cool.

2. In a food processor, combine the butter, sugar, and salt, and process until very smooth and well blended. Add the vanilla and coffee and pulse several times to combine. Add the flour and pulse, scraping down the sides once or twice, just until combined. Add the chocolate and pulse until blended fairly evenly. Some of the chips will get slightly more chopped in the processor, which is what you want. (The dough can also be made with an electric mixer by creaming together the butter, sugar, vanilla, and coffee, and then adding the flour and chopped chocolate.)

3. Scrape the dough into a gallon-size ziplock bag and lay the bag out flat with the top open. Use a rolling pin to roll the dough 1/4 inch thick into a smooth, flat 10-inch square. Lift the bag off the dough to smooth out creases. Seal the bag and refrigerate for at least 2 hours or for up to 2 days.

4. Preheat the oven to 325 degrees. Line two baking sheets with parchment paper.

5. Place the plastic bag on a work surface and slit it down the sides with scissors or a knife. Remove and discard the bag. Use a ruler as a guide and cut the dough into 1½-inch squares. Transfer the cookies to the baking sheets and prick each one, pushing the fork clear down until it hits the baking sheet. Bake for 20 to 22 minutes, rotating the sheets back to front after 10 minutes, until the cookies have lost their shiny look and are almost firm when lightly touched. Transfer to a rack to cool. (Can be stored in a covered container for a couple of days or frozen.)

LOBSTER ICE CREAM

The lobster ice cream at Ben & Bill's Chocolate Emporium is made by folding chopped cooked and buttered lobster meat into vanilla ice cream. Ben and Bill say that one reason they created this unique product was to demonstrate that all of their ice cream is truly homemade. Samples are offered at all their locations in Falmouth, Oak Bluffs, and Northampton, Massachusetts; and Bar Harbor, Maine.

Chocolate Silk Pie

Crust

1 cup graham cracker crumbs (see Note)

3 tablespoons packed light brown sugar

5 tablespoons unsalted butter, melted

~~~~~~~~~~~~~~~~~

Filling

4 ounces semisweet baking chocolate

1/2 cup granulated sugar

1/4 teaspoon salt

3 tablespoons cornstarch

1 1/2 cups whole milk

1 cup heavy cream

6 egg yolks

2 tablespoons unsalted butter, cut into pieces

1 1/2 teaspoons instant coffee or espresso powder

1 teaspoon dark rum

~~~~~~~~~~~~~~~~~

Ingredients continue opposite

Sometimes an old-fashioned chocolate cream pie is exactly the right thing after a lobster dinner. This filling nestles in a toasty graham cracker crust and is smooth as silk and deeply chocolaty.

1. To make the crust, combine the graham cracker crumbs, brown sugar, and melted butter in a bowl and stir with a fork until evenly mixed. Press evenly into the bottom and sides of a 9-inch pie plate. (The back of a spoon or the bottom of a glass works well for pressing.) Refrigerate for at least 20 minutes.

2. Preheat the oven to 350 degrees. Bake the crust for 12 to 15 minutes, until deep golden brown. Cool on a wire rack. Fill immediately or cover and refrigerate for up to 8 hours.

3. To make the filling, heat the chocolate in a microwave, checking and stirring every 30 seconds until melted and smooth. Set aside.

4. In a medium saucepan, whisk together the granulated sugar, salt, and cornstarch. Whisk in about one-third of the milk until smooth. Stir in the remaining milk and the cream, place over medium-high heat and cook, whisking almost constantly, until the mixture thickens and comes just to a boil, 4 to 5 minutes. In a small bowl, lightly beat the egg yolks. Whisk about 1 cup of the hot milk mixture into the yolks to temper them, add the yolk mixture to the saucepan, reduce the heat to medium, and

cook, stirring and scraping the bottom of the pan, until the mixture comes almost back to a boil, about 3 minutes. Remove from the heat and stir in the melted chocolate, butter, coffee powder, and rum. Stir for about 3 minutes to release steam, and then pour the filling into the prepared pie shell. Place a sheet of plastic wrap directly on the surface to prevent a skin from forming and refrigerate until firm, at least 2 to 3 hours. (Can be prepared up to 8 hours ahead.)

5. Before serving, whip the cream with the granulated sugar and vanilla to stiff peaks. Using a pastry bag with a star tip, pipe rosettes on top of the pie or spread the cream in an even layer. Cut into wedges to serve.

NOTE: *Graham cracker crumbs can often be found in the baking section of the supermarket. To make your own, break about 9 full-size graham crackers into pieces and whir in a food processor to make fine crumbs.*

Topping

1 cup heavy cream

2 tablespoons granulated sugar

1 teaspoon vanilla extract

8 SERVINGS

POUNDS, THE EATERIES

Some savvy early-twentieth-century New England fishermen turned their lobster impoundments (pounds) into outdoor eateries. They set up wood-fired cauldrons along the shore so that summer visitors could buy fresh lobsters, watch them cook on the spot, and then settle down at a picnic table for a feast "in-the-rough."

Chocolate Bread and Butter Pudding

with Rum Custard Sauce

Tender, rich chocolate custardy pudding nestles under a lightly glazed crust. Best served warm or lukewarm, the dessert can be made a couple of hours ahead and presented as a grand finale to an important lobster dinner party. You can omit the rum custard sauce but it adds a decadent, lily-gilding finish.

Sauce

1½ cups half-and-half or light cream

3 egg yolks

⅓ cup sugar

¼ teaspoon salt

3 tablespoons dark rum

~~~~~~~~~~~~

Bread Pudding

8 ounces French bread (1 small loaf), preferably day-old

1 tablespoon unsalted butter, softened, for the baking dish

6 ounces semisweet baking chocolate

2 cups heavy cream

1 cup whole milk

4 eggs

¾ cup sugar

Ingredients continue opposite

1. To make the sauce, heat the half-and-half in a saucepan until small bubbles form around the edges. Whisk the egg yolks with the sugar and salt in a medium bowl. Slowly whisk the hot cream into the yolks, and then return the mixture to the saucepan. Cook over medium-low heat, stirring almost constantly, until the custard thickens enough to coat the back of a spoon, about 6 minutes. Pour into a bowl, stir in the rum, and cool for about 20 minutes. Cover and refrigerate for at least 2 hours or for up to 2 days.

2. To make the pudding, cut the bread into ½-inch thick slices and remove the crusts. Smear the butter over the bottom and sides of a 2- to 2½-quart baking dish at least 2 inches deep. Arrange the bread slices in the dish — it's fine to overlap the bread to make it fit.

3. In a saucepan, combine the chocolate and 1 cup of the cream. Place over medium heat and stir frequently until the chocolate is melted and smooth. Add the

remaining 1 cup cream and the milk and heat, stirring, until steam rises, 2 to 3 minutes. Do not boil.

4 Whisk the eggs with the sugar and salt in a large bowl. Slowly whisk in the hot chocolate mixture. Stir in the vanilla. Pour the chocolate custard evenly over the bread, place a sheet of plastic wrap on the surface and place another slightly smaller dish on the plastic wrap. Weight with a couple of cans so the bread is completely immersed in the chocolate custard. Refrigerate for at least 2 hours or overnight.

5 Preheat the oven to 325 degrees.

6 Remove the weights and plastic wrap and cover the baking dish with foil. Place the baking dish in a roasting pan and fill the pan with boiling water to come halfway up the sides of the baking dish. Bake for 20 minutes. Remove the foil and continue to bake for 35 to 45 minutes, until the top is lightly glazed and a knife inserted two-thirds of the way to the center comes out clean. Serve warm or lukewarm, in a pool of custard sauce. (Pudding can be refrigerated overnight. Bring to room temperature and reheat to lukewarm in a microwave or in a 350-degree oven for about 10 minutes.)

⅛ teaspoon salt

2 teaspoons vanilla extract

〰〰〰〰〰〰〰〰

8 SERVINGS

〰〰〰〰〰〰〰〰

INLAND LOBSTER

Not all lobster eateries are located on the coast. Weirs Beach Lobster Pound in Laconia, on New Hampshire's Lake Winnipesaukee, has been in business for over 35 years and still cooks their lobsters in the same specially designed steamer that they've had since the restaurant opened.

〰〰〰〰〰〰〰〰

ACKNOWLEDGMENTS

I live on the Maine coast where lobster fishing permeates the culture. The fishery thrives here, and I am fortunate to be able to buy the freshest possible lobsters right off the dock from the hardworking men (and the occasional woman) who trapped them that day. I gratefully acknowledge them and the following people who helped me with this book:

Cathy Billings, Annette and John Candage, David Chalfant, Ryan Dorr, Bill Dye, John Edwards, Sarah and Tony Everdell, Dick Fenton, Lindsay and Tad Goodale, Barbara Scott Goodman, Bill Grant, Patrick Grant, Rhoda Grant, Sharlene Grant, Nicole Gray, Don and Lee Holmes, Dave Kapell, Barbara and Prep Keyes, Marianne LaCroix, Susan Maloney, Jay Marsh, James Morton, Ginny Olsen, Katherine Hall Page, Wanda Pinkham, Pam and Ralph Siewers, Martha and Charlie Welty, Ned and Brooke Welty.

It is a real pleasure to work with the publishing professionals at Storey, including, especially, Margaret Sutherland and the amazing design team. My agent, Judith Weber, is simply the best!

Many appreciative eaters have joined us over the years at our lobster feasts, but I am most grateful of all to my family, Matt Dojny and Sybil Young, Maury Dojny and Rob Hemphill, and especially Richard.

MAIL ORDER AND INFORMATIONAL WEBSITES

Ben & Bill's Chocolate Emporium
www.benandbills.com
These shops sell lobster ice cream

Big Claw Wine
steve@bigclawwine.com
www.bigclawwine.com
A California white wine blended especially to serve with lobster

David's Fish Market & Lobster Pound
Route 1
Salisbury, MA 01952
978-462-2504
www.davidsfishmarket.com
Fresh seafood of all kinds. Retail only

Duryea's Lobster Deck & Seafood Market
65 Tuthill Road
Montauk, NY 11954
631-668-2410
www.duryealobsters.com
Retail and wholesale seafood and Lobster Deck Restaurant in Montauk, Long Island

iLobster iPhone App
www.ilobsterapp.com
Instructions on how to eat a lobster and other lobster tips

Jasper White's Summer Shack
www.summershackrestaurant.com
Information on the five Summer Shack restaurants in Boston, Cambridge, Dedham, and Hingham, Massachusetts, and at the Mohegan Sun casino in Uncasville, Connecticut

Linda Bean's Maine Lobster
www.lindabeansperfectmaine.com
Updated information on Linda Bean's many businesses, including restaurants, cafes, processing plants, value-added lobster products, and so on

Lobster Institute
207-581-1443
www.lobsterinstitute.org
Based at the University of Maine, the institute works with the lobster industry from New York to Newfoundland, conducting research and providing educational outreach focused on protecting, conserving, and enhancing lobsters and lobstering as an industry, and as a way of life.

Maine Lobster Council
207-541-9310
www.lobsterfrommaine.com
Maintains an up-to-date list of businesses selling live lobsters and lobster meat

BIBLIOGRAPHY

Anderson, Pam. *The Perfect Recipe*. Houghton Mifflin, 1998.

Carpenter, William. *The Wooden Nickel*. Little, Brown and Company, 2002.

Coffin, Robert P. Tristram. *Mainstays of Maine*. Macmillan, 1944.

Connellan, Leo. *The Maine Poems*. Blackberry Books, 1999.

Corson, Trevor. *The Secret Life of Lobsters*. Harper Collins, 2004.

Dojny, Brooke. *Dishing up Maine*. Storey Publishing, 2006.

____. *The New England Clam Shack Cookbook*. Storey Publishing, 2008.

____. *The New England Cookbook*. Harvard Common Press, 1999.

Garten, Ina. *Barefoot Contessa Back to Basics*. Clarkson Potter, 2008.

Gilbert, Elizabeth. *Stern Men*. Houghton Mifflin, 2000.

Greenlaw, Linda. *The Lobster Chronicles*. Hyperion, 2002.

Greenlaw, Linda, and Martha Greenlaw. *Recipes from a Very Small Island*. Hyperion, 2005.

Greenspan, Dorie. *Baking: From My Home to Yours*. Houghton Mifflin, 2006.

Killeen, Johanne, and George Germon. *Cucina Simpatica*. HarperCollins, 1991.

King, Richard. *Lobster*. Reaktion Books, 2011.

Oliver, Sandy. www.foodhistorynews.com.

Rombauer, Irma S., Marion Rombauer Becker, and Ethan Becker. *The 1997 Joy of Cooking*. Scribner, 1997.

Rosso, Julee, Sheila Lukins, McLaughlin, Michael. *The Silver Palate Cookbook*. Workman, 1982.

White, Jasper. *Jasper White's Cooking from New England*. Harper and Row, 1989.

____. *Lobster at Home*. Scribner, 1998.

____. *The Summer Shack Cookbook*. W.W. Norton, 2007.

Woodard, Colin. *The Lobster Coast*. Viking, 2004.

INDEX

Page references in *italics* indicate photos or illustrations; page references in **bold** indicate charts.

Other Storey Titles You Will Enjoy

Also by Brooke Dojny:

DISHING UP MAINE

A delicious journey through the foodways of the Pine Tree State —
from fresh seafood and to blueberries and maple syrup.
288 pages. Paper. ISBN 978-1-58017-841-9.

THE NEW ENGLAND CLAM SHACK COOKBOOK, 2ND EDITION

A culinary tribute to New England seafood traditions, with nearly
100 recipes gathered from eateries up and down the coast.
256 pages. Paper. ISBN 978-1-60342-026-6.

DISHING UP MARYLAND, by Lucie L. Snodgrass.

Food lore, travel advice, fascinating profiles of chefs, farmers, and fishermen,
and 150 recipes from the Old Line State.
288 pages. Paper. ISBN 978-1-60342-527-8.

FISH GRILLED & SMOKED, by John Manikowski.

One hundred and fifty recipes for preparing fresh and saltwater fish in the
kitchen and at the campsite.
264 pages. Paper. ISBN 978-1-58017-502-9.

MAPLE SUGAR, by Tim Herd.

From sap to syrup: the history, lore, and how-to behind this sweet treat.
144 pages. Paper. ISBN 978-1-60342-735-7.

PICNIC, by DeeDee Stovel.

A cornucopia of seasonal picnic ideas, from the informal to the elegant, plus
more than 125 recipes for soups, salads, entrées, and desserts.
192 pages. Paper. ISBN 978-1-58017-377-3.

These and other books from Storey Publishing are available
wherever quality books are sold or by calling 1-800-441-5700.
Visit us at www.storey.com.